GLORY

AND THE

GAMES

ALLSPORT/JONES

ALLSPORT/BRUTY

ALLSPORT/RONDEAU

COMMEMORATIVE PUBLICATIONS
SALT LAKE CITY, UTAH

publisher
Mikko S. Laitinen
Commemorative
Publications, Inc.

marketing manager
Kari M. Laitinen

managing editor
Lisa H. Albertson

profiles
Lee Benson, Doug
Robinson, Dee Benson

typesetting
Marjo Peltonen

cover design
Mike Light, Jess Clifford

ALLSPORT/STEWART

USOC contributors
John Krimsky, Jr.
Deputy Secretary General
Barry King
Director of Marketing and Communications
Mike Moran
Asst. Exec. Director, Media and Public Affairs
Frank Zang
Editor
C. Robert Paul
Editorial Consultant

photography
Allsport Photography,
Los Angeles and London
Sport Museum of Finland, Helsinki

printing
Banta ISG
Spanish Fork, Utah

color separations
Pre Press Services, Inc.
Salt Lake City

paper
Westvaco
Sterling 100 lb. Gloss

ink
Flint Ink Corporation
Detroit, Salt Lake City

ALLSPORT/COLE

special thanks
Orris E. Albertson, Sue Baldus, Banta
Spanish Fork staff, Ken Bell, Charles F.
Carlson, Robert Colson, Dwayne Dyer,
Fred Gruter, Judd Parr, Tom Kupka, Sarah
Laitinen, Tarja Laitinen, Doug Norton,
Steve Stolba, Dee Thompson, Peter
Vidmar, Jeff N. Walker, Bill White

The publisher, on behalf of the authors,
would like to pay particular thanks to the
staff of the Los Angeles Amateur Athletic
Foundation for their invaluable research
assistance. They include Wayne Wilson,
vice president, research; librarians Shirley
Ito and Michael Salmon; and library
assistant Bonita Carter.

**Published under license from the
U.S. Olympic Committee by:**
Commemorative Publications, Inc.
P.O. Box 71038
Salt Lake City, UT 84171
tel (801) 288-9668
fax (801) 262-6883
The editorial materials contained in *Glory and The Games* are
produced by Commemorative Publications exclusively and are
not the responsibility of the U.S. Olympic Committee.

ISBN 0-918883-09-1

ALLSPORT/BOTTERILL

FOREWORD

by Peter Vidmar

Double gold medalist,
men's gymnastics,
Los Angeles, 1984

Inducted into United States
Olympic Hall of Fame, 1991

I had my game face on.

Less than two weeks remained before the start of the 1984 Olympic Games in Los Angeles and I was in the final stages of preparation — easing back on my workouts, eating right, emphasizing rest, and, above all else, doing everything I could not to psyche myself out.

Which is why I was determined to ignore any and all gold medals.

I didn't want to see a gold medal, I didn't want to touch a gold medal, I didn't want to *hear* about a gold medal.

Some people would have called it superstitious. I called it scared.

But even the best intended of game plans can go awry, and so it was with this one when I found myself reporting to a meeting inside the First Interstate Athletic Foundation offices on the corner of Adams and Gramercy Streets in my hometown of Los Angeles, a.k.a. Olympic City.

I turned the corner and there, directly in front of me, was an Olympic exhibit.

Before I could turn away, my eyes riveted on the four gold medals won by swimmer John Naber in Montreal in 1976. *You're not supposed to look*, I thought to myself, but I kept looking anyway, powerless to do otherwise. I stared at Naber's medals for a long time and then I turned to the other medals and Olympic memorabilia on display.

I had been a big fan of the Olympics as far back as I could remember, so I was familiar with much of what I was seeing. What I hadn't watched personally on television I'd absorbed by immersing myself in Bud Greenspan's terrific Olympic documentaries. I was an avid student of the legends, the incredible stories, the inspirational endings, and now I was soaking it all in, binging on the lore.

When I saw the display for Al Oerter, I knew I was looking at a tribute to "Mr. Olympics," a man who managed to win four gold medals in four consecutive Olympics even though he wasn't supposed to.

As I stood in front of that exhibit in the lobby, the magic and glamour of the Games grabbed and mesmerized me. This was way bigger than I was.

Although I thought just the opposite would happen, seeing those medals didn't hurt but instead aided my mental preparation, further strengthening a resolve that, before the month was out, would help me and my American teammates win the first men's gymnastics team gold medal in U.S. history, and inspire me to go on and add gold and silver medals in the individual competition.

The Olympic movement *is* its history. Without its inspiring past, it would have no inspiring future.

Glory and The Games is about helping to preserve that history, to ensure the Olympic legacy. What Bud Greenspan has done with his films, Commemorative Publications and Lee Benson have done with this publication.

If you're the young aspiring athlete, looking for inspiration, for role models, for proof it can be done, read the stories in these pages and let them inspire you to glory. If your pursuits are outside the athletic arena, adapt these contents to your own particular goals and purposes.

The Olympic ideal of *Citius, Altius, Fortius* — Faster, Higher, Stronger — is universally applicable. Whatever your obstacles and challenges, your hopes and your dreams, chances are you will find their match here. ▼

In Atlanta, Jani Sievinen held the title of world-record holder in the 200-meter individual medley, but on race day, he was upset by Attila Czene of Hungary.
ALLSPORT/BRUTY

Taking a breather. ALLSPORT/RONDEAU

In Atlanta, Russia and Brazil (pictured) bandied it out for the bronze, won by Brazil, while Cuba, the defending Olympic champion, beat China, 3-1, for the gold in women's volleyball.

GREETINGS FROM THE U.S. OLYMPIC COMMITTEE

Our Vision

The U.S. Olympic Committee is dedicated to preparing America's athletes to represent the United States in the ongoing pursuit and achievement of excellence in the Olympic Games and in life.

Our Olympians inspire Americans, particularly our youth, to embrace Olympic ideals and to pursue excellence in sport and in their lives.

Our Mission

What is the USOC? The United States Olympic Committee is an organization mandated by Congress under the Amateur Sports Act of 1978, to govern Olympic and Pan American Games-related activities in the USA. The USOC represents athletes, coaches and administrators of Olympic sport, and the American people who support the Olympic movement.

The USOC is committed to diversity. This means encouraging and recruiting diverse participation in the USOC as an organization, as well as in sports.

Making Dreams Come True

More than 25,000 athletes prepare for their competitive endeavors each year at the Olympic Training and Education Centers.

It is the responsibility of the National Governing Body to administer all coaching and technical training support for its respective athletes using the training centers. The USOC offers the athletes free room and board, training facilities, sports medicine care, sport science testing and anaylsis, local transportation and recreational facilities.

Colorado Springs OTC

Opened in July of 1977, the Colorado Springs OTC has undergone over $37 million in renovations including a state-of-the-art aquatics center that opened in 1993.

Lake Placid OTC

Originally opened in 1982 and renovated in 1989, the Lake Placid OTC is located on a 29-acre parcel and has facilities for all of the winter sports.

ARCO Training Center

The $42 million ARCO Training Center in Chula Vista, Calif., opened its doors in April of 1995 thanks to two major contributors: ARCO Corporation, which donated $15 million to the project, and the East Lake Development Company, which donated the 150 acres of land.

Marquette OEC

As an Olympic Education Center, Northern Michigan University allows Olympic-caliber athletes to train for a sport and to attend school. Athletes who participate in the program pay in-state tuition and are allowed to use the athletic facilities on the NMU campus.

In addition, the USOC has designated three other Olympic training facilities for yachting, speed skating and equestrian.

The U.S. Sailing Center, located in Miami, opened in September of 1996 with a 15-year lease agreement.

The $13.3 million Pettit Center in Milwaukee has an indoor 400-meter speed skating oval.

The U.S. Equestrian Team Training Facility in Gladstone, N.J., has three permanent barns and 500 acres of land.

For more information, call the Olympic tour and events hotline at 1-888-OLY-TOUR or visit our website at www.usolympic.org.

COLORADO SPRINGS OTC, COURTESY OF THE USOC

USOC Member Organizations

Olympic Sport Organizations (37)

National Archery Association
USA Badminton
USA Baseball
USA Basketball
U.S. Biathlon Association
U.S. Bobsled and Skeleton Fed.
USA Boxing
American Canoe Association
   U.S. Canoe and Kayak Team
USA Curling
USA Cycling, Inc.
United States Diving, Inc.
American Horse Shows Association
   U.S. Equestrian Team
U.S. Fencing Association
U.S. Field Hockey Association
U.S. Figure Skating Association
USA Gymnastics
USA Hockey, Inc.
United States Judo, Inc.
U.S. Luge Association
U.S. Modern Pentathlon Association
United States Rowing Assoc. (U.S. Rowing)
United States Sailing Assoc. (U.S. Sailing)
USA Shooting
U.S. Ski and Snowboard Association
U.S. Soccer Federation
Amateur Softball Association
U.S. Speedskating
U.S. Swimming, Inc.
U.S. Synchronized Swimming, Inc.
USA Table Tennis
U.S. Team Handball Federation
U.S. Tennis Association
USA Track and Field
USA Volleyball
United States Water Polo
USA Weightlifting
USA Wrestling

Pan American Sport Organizations (6)

USA Bowling
United States Racquetball Association
USA Roller Skating
U.S. Squash Racquets Association
*U.S. Taekwondo Union
American Water Ski Association

Affiliated Sport Organizations (6)

#United States of America National
   Karate-Do Federation, Inc.
U.S. Orienteering Federation
United States Sports Acrobatics Federation
USA Trampoline and Tumbling
*USA Triathlon Federation
Underwater Society of America

Community-based Multisport Organizations (12)

Amateur Athletic Union
American Alliance for Health,
   Physical Ed., Recreation and Dance
Boys and Girls Clubs of America
Catholic Youth Organization
Jewish Community Centers Association
Nat'l Assoc. of Police Athletic Leagues, Inc.
National Congress of State Games
National Exploring Division, Boy Scouts
   of America
Native American Sports Council
U.S. National Senior Sport Organization
YMCA of the USA
YWCA of the USA

Education-based Multisport Organizations (4)

Nat'l Assoc. of Intercollegiate Athletics (NAIA)
National Collegiate Athletic Assoc. (NCAA)
National Federation of State High School
   Associations (NFSHSA)
National Junior College Athletic Association
   (NJCAA)

Armed Forces (1)

U.S. Armed Forces Sports

Disabled in Sports (7)

American Athletic Assoc. of the Deaf, Inc.
U.S. Cerebral Palsy Athletic Association
Disabled Sports USA
Dwarf Athletic Assoc. of America
Wheelchair Sports USA
Special Olympics International
U.S. Association for Blind Athletes

*Taekwondo and triathlon are on the medal program of the 2000 Olympic Games in Sydney, Australia. The U.S. Taekwondo Union's request to be elevated to an Olympic Sport Organization member is under review by the USOC Membership and Credentials Committee. USA Triathlon is on the USOC Board of Directors' November 1998 agenda and is expected to be elevated to Olympic Sport Organization status at that meeting.

#Karate is on the medal program of the 1999 Pan American Games in Winnipeg, Canada.

William J. Hybl,
President

Richard D. Schultz,
Executive Director

The USOC is governed by a volunteer Board of Directors and Executive Committee. The USOC is managed by an Executive Director with a paid professional staff.

USOC Officers

William J. Hybl, *President*
Sandra Baldwin, *Vice President*
Herman Frazier, *Vice President*
Paul E. George, *Vice President*
Andrew Kostanecki, *Secretary*
James T. Morris, *Treasurer*

USOC Executive Office

Richard D. Schultz,
Executive Director

John Krimsky, Jr.,
Deputy Secretary General and Managing Director, Business Affairs

Tom Wilkinson,
Assistant Executive Director

Jim Page,
Deputy Executive Director for Programs

ALLSPORT/M. POWELL

In the super G (pictured), Katja Seizinger ended her medals hopes with a crash, but the German silenced the critics and roared back to form with a flawless gold-medal downhill run in Lillehammer. ALLSPORT/COLE

IN THE BEGINNING

L ike most idea men, Pierre de Coubertin did not have it easy. Yes, he was born to money. Yes, he was royalty. And yes, he did jump start the Olympic Games, taking to heart those now famous words: "The important thing in the Olympic Games is not winning but taking part. Just as in life, the aim is not to conquer but to struggle well."

His was a life largely spent wrestling with that curse common to people of vision: Trying to get others to see what they are seeing.

This, after all, was a frail Frenchman born on New Year's Day, 1863, who revived the greatest athletic tradition in the history of the world – and how incongruous is that? When the young Coubertin was growing up in and around Paris in the latter part of the nineteenth century, the French looked at "physical" educators with only slightly less scorn than those who still considered the earth flat.

Not much of an athletic practitioner himself – he stood 5-foot-3 and, even when his enormous handlebar mustache was in full growth, barely exceeded a hundred pounds in weight – Coubertin nonetheless ignored the derision of his countrymen as he doggedly subscribed to the notion that the universal pursuit of sport was the answer to breaking down barriers between nations and their peoples. The pathway to peace and harmony, in other words. The ancient Greeks, he firmly believed, were on to something with their Games.

Family clout

HE TOOK HIS INFLUENCES FROM ANY-where and everywhere – from the German archaeologists who excavated the ancient Greek city of Olympia in the 1880s; from the English educators who pioneered the establishment of sport as the core of their curriculum; even from the Americans, barely beyond their own civil war, who contributed their own independent input concerning the place of sport. As a young man, Coubertin dipped into the family fortune to travel extensively and thus absorbed all this "influence" – to England first, then America, and finally to Olympia, where he stood amid the excavated ruins of Zeus' temple and soaked in enough inspiration to see him through a lifetime of people constantly informing him that he was, if not crazy, at the very least eccentric.

Where the drive, and the rebelliousness, came from, who knew? Certainly not from his father, who despaired as his son first dropped out of military school and then, at the age of 21, out of law school as well, thereafter to become, for the want of a better description, a statesman for sportsmen – and a self-appointed one, at that.

Pierre's father expected something more *acceptable* from a son of privilege. The Coubertin's aristocracy dated back to 1477 – when Louis XI enobled a long-ago Coubertin who served the king as chamberlain – and in the 400 years until *Baron* Pierre came along, the family chain was filled with military officers, barristers, and the occasional diplomat.

But if Pierre didn't have his father's, or his family's, full-fledged support, he had the Coubertin family clout – clout that enabled him to set up his various symposiums and conferences at offices at the prestigious Sorbonne outside of Paris.

Follow that dream

It was at the Sorbonne that Coubertin first publicly revealed his brainstorm to revive the ancient Olympic Games, dormant now some fifteen hundred years. First in a speech in 1892, when he was jeered back to his seat, and again in 1894, at the International Athletics Congress (grandly named by Coubertin himself), where sportsmen from a dozen nations finally squared

But of course it was never that simple. The truth is, the Father of the Games slugged it out with conventional wisdom all of his natural life, wet-nursing his cause through potential disaster after potential disaster, breathing it back to life time and again. It was Coubertin who talked the first Games into Greece, and then, afraid a permanent host would end their universal appeal, who massaged them back out; it was Coubertin who talked everyone back to the table after

Olympian at heart

He was competitive, innovative, resourceful, relentless – and he never lost his focus. He overcame adversity, piles of it; time and again he engineered impressive comebacks; and, in the process, he turned himself into a legendary figure, a star in his own right. In short, throughout his life the Baron de Coubertin developed and exhibited all the qualities of an Olympic champion.

ALLSPORT/BRUTY

The important thing in the Olympic Games is not winning
but taking part.
Just as in life,
the aim is
not to conquer
but to struggle well.

themselves in their plush velvet chairs long enough to actually *listen* to what the small Baron at the podium had to say.

The vote to give the revival a try was unanimous.

A lifetime pursuit

It's easy to say "the rest is history," now that the Olympic movement has survived two world wars, any number of insurrections, boycotts, scandals, the political-social meddlings of, among others, Adolf Hitler himself – and now that Pierre de Coubertin is a household name, toasted by billions, the universally acknowledged Father of the Modern Olympics.

misguided partnerships with world expositions in Paris and St. Louis; it was Coubertin who jumped between the Brits and the Yanks after the tumultuous London Games of 1908; it was Coubertin who moved the Olympic headquarters from Paris to the neutral safety of Lausanne, Switzerland, just before the outbreak of World War I; it was Coubertin who made sure the Olympics rebounded quickly after that war, reconvening in, of all places, wartorn Antwerp, where the contrast between peaceful competition and the destruction of warfare would not be easily missed – or dismissed; and it was Coubertin who, in the end, managed to go broke in the process.

All he ever lacked was an official event.

The thirty-nine stories that follow are about Olympians who, thanks to Pierre de Coubertin, *did not* lack for an official event. They are stories that also tell of overcoming adversity, of engineering impressive comebacks, and of becoming stars. Stories – some well-known, others less so – that testify that the spirit of the uncommon man who revived the Games – who *struggled well* – permeates them still.

More than a century later, this book pays tribute and is dedicated to Pierre de Coubertin's extraordinary vision, both that part we can now see clearly ... and the part we're yet to bring into focus. ▼

Spain put away Pakistan, 3-0, early in the tournament, but any gold-medal hopes were dashed by the dominant Dutch men, who concluded their Atlanta run with a 6-0-1 record. ALLSPORT/FORSTER

Say a little prayer for me. France's Cedric Plancon competes in the 90-kilogram (198 pounds) division in Barcelona. The event was won by Kakhi Kakhiachvili of the Unified Team, which captured five of the 10 golds in weightlifting.
ALLSPORT/BOTTERILL

When Carl Lewis debuted in 1984 in Los Angeles, his four gold-medal performance drew comparisons to the legendary Jesse Owens, who also won four gold medals in the same events in Berlin in 1936. Lewis went on to become his own legend competing in three more Olympic Games and collecting 10 Olympic medals, nine golds, one silver. ALLSPORT/CANNON

In Barcelona, the 50-meter freestyle, in only its third Olympic appearance (also 1904 and 1988) showcased the event's world-record holders: Alexander Popov of Russia, Matt Biondi of the U.S. and teammate Tom Jager (pictured). Popov won in 17 strokes breaking the 22-second barrier with Biondi in second and Jager in third. Both Biondi and Jager earned the distinction of being the first U.S. swimmers to win a gold medal in three different Olympic Games when they helped the 4x100-meter freestyle relay team to victory. **ALLSPORT/BRUTY**

With a war raging in Bosnia-Herzegovina, the four-man bobsled team was a bright spot in Lillehammer, where few Bosnian athletes were able to travel much less train for their sport. The Bosnians finished in last place. ALLSPORT/M. POWELL

OVERCOMING
ADVERSITY

"Life is simple because
the fight is simple.
The good fighter retreats,
but never runs away;
he gives ground
but never gives up ...
And even when
everything is crumbling
around him,
he still refuses
to give up hope."

Pierre de Coubertin,
Olympic Almanach, 1918

They are the stories that provide the heart and soul of the Olympic Games. Stories of conquering, of subduing, of vanquishing, of staring down the odds. Stories that boost, encourage, lift, motivate, and inspire. Stories that make you feel better every time you hear them.

They are stories that serve as reminders that the human spirit is not just indomitable, but that being indomitable is hardly a modern invention. That there's nothing original about courage. That tales of "hurdling obstacles" date back to the very origins of the Olympic Games, both modern and ancient.

When gymnast Kerri Strug inhales as much oxygen as possible and then takes off down the Atlanta runway for her vault, her ankle screaming at her to stop but her sense of duty screaming at her not to, she's going where Shun Fujimoto, dismounting from the rings in Montreal on a broken kneecap, went some 20 years before. When Wilma Rudolph stands tall and proud on a victory podium in Rome, proof positive that the crippling diseases of childhood can be overcome if you work hard enough and don't feel sorry for yourself, she's going where high jumper Walt Davis, who spent part of the third grade in a polio ward, went before. When swimmer Amy Van Dyken, asthmatic, hauls in her fourth swimming gold medal in Atlanta, she's going the same place weightlifter Tommy Kono, asthmatic, went when he collected medals in three straight Olympic Games in three different weight classes, and they're both visiting where swimmer Johnny Weissmuller, asthmatic, had already been. When equestrian Lis Hartel competes without a leg, she's Hungarian shooter Karoly Takacs shooting without a hand. When 30-year-old Irena Szewinska overcomes youth and childbirth and wins the 400-meter run in Montreal, she's Gretchen Fraser, a week from 29, overcoming youth and a world war to win the slalom at St. Moritz. And when Agnes Keleti ignores the ravages of Adolf Hitler – whose oppression once sent her to exile in France and her father to death at Auschwitz – to carry on and shine in the Aussie Games of 1956, she's Jesse Owens all over again.

They are stories of the human spirit that do not grow old; they are for the ages. ▼

In Lillehammer, where the passion for Nordic sports runs feverishly high, the men's 4x10-kilometer cross country relay race turned from party to wake when Italy's Silvio Fauner outlegged Norway's Bjorn Daehlie by two strides and four-tenths of a second for the gold medal.

ALLSPORT/RONDEAU

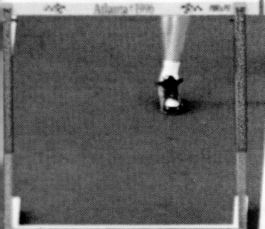
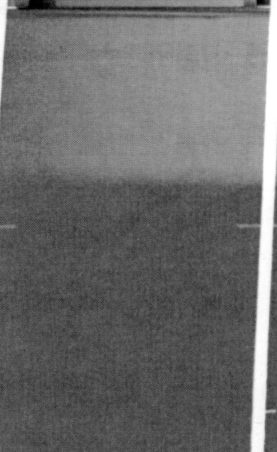

From semifinals (pictured) to the final race, Allen Johnson led the field in the 110-meter hurdles in Atlanta. He set an Olympic record of 12.95 seconds despite knocking down several hurdles.

A   l   b   e   r   t   .   H   i   l   l

OVER THE HILL?

When 31-year-old Albert Hill showed up at the track for the 1920 Olympic Games in Antwerp, Belgium, they didn't call him "Over the Hill" Hill.

At least not to his face.

But behind the scenes, there was a good deal of talk among "the youth of the world" concerning the British runner's advanced years. Albert George Hill was a veteran in every sense of the word. Not only did his days as a competitive runner stretch back to the early 1900s – when he found his stride as a teenager and captured some of Britain's most prestigious youth championships, including the 1909 North of the Thames cross-country championship – but Hill was also a "veteran" in the armed services sense of the word. From 1916 through 1919, he had served in France as a wireless operator with the Royal Flying Corps of Great Britain's Royal Air Force. For better than three long years, Hill's "training" consisted of crawling from trench to trench over the war-torn turf of La

Sienne and Normandy, dodging German bullets. Only when the Germans were defeated and the war ended did he re-cross the English Channel and return to his native London.

But whereas most of England's World War I vets, set up for life with war sto-

> If he went for the "middle distance double" by competing in both the 800-meter and 1,500-meter events, the members of the selection committee argued that the pace would be too taxing "for a man of his age."

ries and their country's thanks, chose to retire to a more sedentary lifestyle, Lieutenant Hill was bound and determined to pick up where he left off. At 30 years of age, and with conventional wisdom suggesting that his best running days, and times, were well behind him, he

secured the services of England's best track coach, Sam Mussabini, and set out to find his old stride.

He seemed to find it, too, when he won the British Amateur Athletic Association championships at both 880 yards and the mile just weeks after his return from France. After those flashes of triumph, however, reality seemed to set in and by a year later at the 1920 AAA championships – which served as a preview for the upcoming Olympic Games – Hill didn't even enter the mile and could only finish second in the 880 where he was outclassed by a much heralded, and much younger, runner from South Africa named Bevil Rudd.

In the aftermath of that meet, Britain's selectors for the Antwerp Olympics, led by AAA secretary Sir Harry Barclay, lobbied against Hill's inclusion in any more than one race at the Games. If he went for the "middle distance double" by competing in both the 800-meter and 1,500-meter events, the members of the selection committee argued that the pace would be too taxing "for a man of his age." By trying to do too much, he would hurt his own chances, they said, and Britain's as well.

The selectors might have prevailed if not for one significant factor: In the summer of 1920, the war was still a keen memory, and an open wound, in the minds of most Britons, and veterans were very much a favored species. It turned out that Hill's British teammates, upon learning of his desire to "go for two," shouted the selectors down, lobbying for the war hero among them. If he wanted to run in both the 800 and 1,500 in Belgium – a country decimated by the war that was nonetheless selected as the Olympic host purely on the basis of paying tribute to a land that gave its all to the war effort – then let him.

And indeed, when Hill arrived in Belgium, it seemed he and Antwerp were made for each other. Both had seen better days. The Antwerp track, resurrected only a few months before the Games from war ruins, was barely serviceable, its cinders lumpy and uneven, its footing treacherous. The stadium itself was in similar shape. As for Hill, after a stormy, tumultuous crossing over the English Channel, he wound up missing the official British transport that took the bulk of the team to the stadium. Wearing his uniform, he had to hitch a ride to the track in a truck, barely arriving in time for his opening heat in the 800.

Still, the conditions were better than anything he'd ever seen in France ...

He breezed through that opening 800-meter heat, and again through the second round, qualifying into the finals where the medal favorites included 25-year-old Earl Eby of the United States, 19-year-old Edgar Mountain of Great Britain, and 25-year-old Rudd, the brash and confident South African.

Hill had a whole new crop of younger runners ready to gun him down. This time the favorites were 23-year-old Sven Lundgren of Sweden, 26-year-old U.S. national champion Joie Ray, and 25-year-old American Lawrence Shields. For most of the race, run in the face of a steady rain, Hill ran just off the lead, in fourth place, flanked the whole while by British teammate and fellow World War I vet,

ing the bronze to Shields. Once again, experience and wile had prevailed over youth and speed.

Since those Games of 1920, only Peter Snell, the great New Zealand middle-distance runner, has managed to equal Hill's "double," when he produced wins at both 800 and 1,500 meters in the 1964 Olympic Games in Tokyo. In an enduring

Undaunted, Hill stayed in a pack with the younger men, and on the final straightaway surprised them all as he surged to a kick that left them all behind. He beat Eby by two-tenths of a second, with Rudd a step behind in third and Mountain another step back in fourth.

Two days later, in the finals of the 1,500,

31-year-old Philip Baker. It appeared the 800 had taken its expected toll.

But on the gun lap, Hill stretched to the front as Baker shielded him from any serious attacks. The two Brits, 62 years between them, strategically drafted their way to the finish line, where they comfortably took the gold and the silver, leaving the bronze to Shields.

tribute to his endurance, at 31, Albert Hill remains the oldest winner of either race in Olympic history. ▼

ABOVE / *At age 31, Albert Hill of England won both the 800- and 1,500-meter races at Antwerp, making him the oldest Olympic champion to accomplish this feat.* ALLSPORT

The women's point race, a whirl of colors as riders jockeyed for position, made its Olympic debut in Atlanta at Stone Mountain. The race was won by Nathalie Lancien of France. French riders dominated in Atlanta, winning nine medals overall, five golds, three silvers and one bronze. ALLSPORT/RONDEAU

Johnny . Weissmuller

JOHNNY BE GOOD

L ittle Johnny was anemic, sickly and 11 years old when the doctor suggested he might try swimming to strengthen his weakened heart.

The doctor had no idea he was speaking to Tarzan.

Then again, neither did Little Johnny.

Few athletes, Olympian or otherwise, can boast of getting more out of a sport than Johnny Weissmuller got out of swimming. First it cleared up his health. Then it got him to the top of the Olympic podium – not once, but five times. And after that it got him to a movie career, swinging from vine to vine as the most famous jungle character of all time.

Through it all, Johnny Weissmuller, a.k.a. Tarzan, was able to set a standard for turning Olympic gold into, well, gold. In most respects, he was the first Olympian of the modern era to translate success and visibility in the Olympic arena into post-Olympic fame and fortune. Whereas the likes of Jim Thorpe, who won the pentathlon and decathlon in the 1912 Games; Ray Ewry, who won a

record 10 jumping medals from 1896 through 1906; Paavo Nurmi, who started his spectacular Olympic run with three gold medals in the 1920 Games, and dozens of other stars of the early Olympics who tended to either go on to other sporting activities or quietly return

> "Swear to me you'll stay with me a year and do what I say," he said. "You won't swim against anybody, you'll be a slave and you'll hate my guts. But in the end you might break every record there is."
>
> — Bill Bachrach
> former U.S. Olympic
> Team swimming coach

to their private lives, it was Weissmuller who first showed that it was possible to wring yet more public success in pursuits totally apart from athletics. As Tarzan, and later as Jungle Jim, he became a certifiable "matinee idol," turning himself into an actor equally as famous, if not more so, than he'd ever been as a swimmer. Indeed, throughout his very public life Weissmuller alternately shocked fans

of his swimming, who were amazed when they discovered that he was Tarzan, and fans of his movies, who were just as amazed to learn that their jungle hero was an Olympic champion.

Not that Weissmuller planned any of it. He didn't become a swimmer with the Olympics in mind any more than he became an Olympian with a movie career in mind. His was a life of one opportunity *always* leading to another.

He might never have learned to swim at all if not for that doctor in his youth, who recommended the exercise for the frail youngster plagued by heart trouble and anemia. Johnny and his older brother, who lived on the poor side of Chicago with their immigrant mother (their father, a coal miner, died early of tuberculosis), decided to give it a try. Since they didn't have access to any swimming pools, they simply dove into Lake Michigan. It was there, in the lake's cold waters, that Johnny, fighting the strong currents, discovered a natural affinity for swimming.

His heart and body did, in fact, benefit, to the point that he could win races at will, both in the lake and later at the local YMCA. It was at the YMCA that he caught the attention of Bill Bachrach, the coach of the Illinois Athletic Club and former United States Olympic Team swimming coach. One glance and the coach was in awe of the teenager's talent, if not his stroke. He pulled Weissmuller aside. "Swear to me you'll stay with me a year and do what I say," he said. "You won't swim against anybody, you'll be a slave and you'll hate my guts. But in the end you might break every record there is."

Johnny said OK.

By the time he was 17 years old, Weissmuller set his first world record. There would be 50 more before he was through. At 18, he became the first person in history to swim 100 meters in less than a minute, and finally, a month after he turned 20, he qualified for his first Olympics, setting sail for the 1924 Games in Paris.

Antwerp. At 34, Kahanamoku was well past his prime, but his specter lingered nonetheless, and it wasn't until Weissmuller relegated the revered Duke to second place, defeating him by more than two seconds, that both a physical and symbolic passing of the crown took place. Suddenly, Chicago's Johnny Weissmuller was the world's fastest swimmer.

two more gold medals – at 100 meters and again in the relay – but was also chosen to carry the United States flag in the Opening Ceremonies.

He was favored to do more of the same in the 1932 Games in Los Angeles, but it was then that commerce intervened. The BVD company asked the Olympic hero to model its swimming suits in magazine ads for five years at $500 a week – unheard-of money at the start of the Great Depression – and although it would end his days as an amateur (and, hence, an Olympian), Weissmuller readily agreed. When MGM movie executives saw the ads, they invited Weissmuller to Hollywood to audition for the lead role in their upcoming movie, *Tarzan, the Ape Man*. And although Weissmuller had exactly zero acting experience, he landed the part, which he called, "Perfect: You swim a lot and you don't say much."

He would make a dozen full-length films, from 1932 through 1948, before his run as Tarzan was through. He wound up bequeathing the role, appropriately enough, to three other Olympians, shot-putter Herman Brix, swimmer Buster Crabbe, and decathlete Glenn Morris – men who, once Johnny Weissmuller showed them the way, were more than eager to follow in his wake. ▼

For his first act in Paris, he defeated the most famous 400-meter freestyler in history, world record-holder Arne Borg of Sweden. That set up a showdown two days later in the showcase 100-meter final against an even larger legend, the great Duke Kahanamoku of Hawaii, winner of the 100 at both the 1912 Games in Stockholm and the 1920 Games in

Weissmuller added to his Paris medal collection by helping the U.S. 4x200 relay team to a gold medal and by competing, in his spare time, with the U.S. water polo team that won the bronze medal. The four medals were more than enough to set up hero status that carried into the 1928 Games in Amsterdam, where the versatile Weissmuller not only won

LEFT / *Johnny Weissmuller, who went on to become a matinee idol playing Tarzan, won a total of six Olympic medals — five gold medals in swimming, three in 1924 and two in 1928, and one bronze as part of the 1924 water polo team.* ALLSPORT/USOC

Two years before Barcelona, Gail Devers overcame
Graves' disease and a near amputation of her feet.
She had already won the 100 meters and, as the
pre-race favorite, she cruised through the semifinal
race (pictured) in the 100-meter hurdles, but the
final hurdle in the final race proved to be her
undoing. Devers crawled to the finish line in fifth.
ALLSPORT/M. POWELL

Pint-size Dominique Moceanu of the U.S. flies through the air with the greatest of ease. She, along with her teammates, won the gold in the team competition in gymnastics in Atlanta. At the other end of the size spectrum is super heavyweight Andrey Chermerkin of Russia (opposite), who celebrates his gold-medal victory. Strapped financially, just getting to Atlanta was a weight off his shoulders. **ALLSPORT/BRUTY**

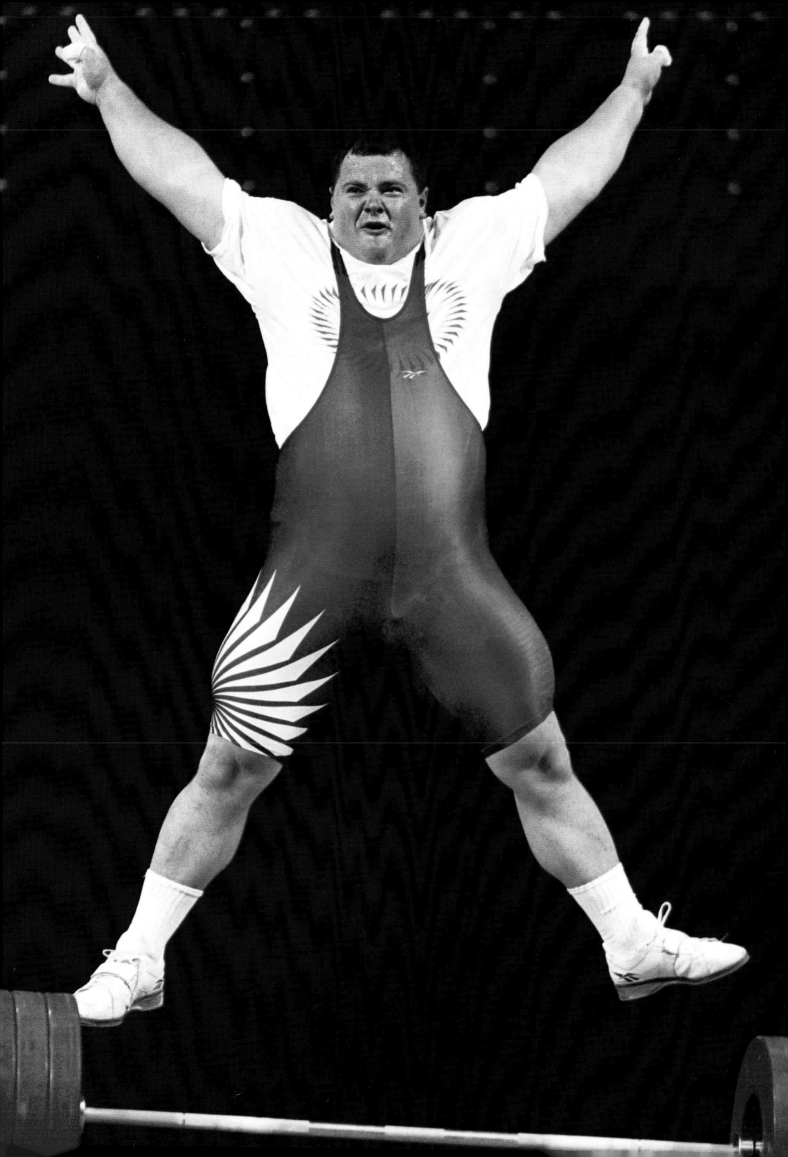

J e s s e . O w e n s

THE PEACE MAKER

Jesse Owens versus Adolf Hitler. As Olympiads come and go, it remains the quintessential Olympic showdown. In one corner, *Der Fuhrer*, determined to use the Olympic Games as a vehicle for social and political purposes. In the other corner, *The Ebony Antelope*, bound and determined to, well, run and jump.

One had an agenda crammed with objectives, goals and ulterior motives; the other had a pair of track shoes. One wanted to conquer the world and suppress human rights; the other had already conquered the world, in a record-breaking kind of way, and was happy to let one and all take their shots at him. One didn't want to shake hands. The other wanted to shake hands with everyone.

Somehow, the fates conspired to bring them together ... in the summer of 1936 ... in Berlin, Germany.

They never did meet face to face, at least not up close. In his memoirs, Owens said he thought he saw Hitler smiling and waving to him as he made his way up the stadium steps after he'd won at 100

meters in his first event of the Berlin Games – and Jesse, instinctively, waved and smiled back. But he later reconsidered what he thought he saw, after the German chancellor excused himself from the stadium prior to any victory ceremonies, including Jesse's four.

Certainly Hitler made no effort to hide his disdain regarding the black race – Jesse's race – in general. In the months

In the space of a week in Berlin in 1936, it was Jesse Owens who redefined the Olympic Games as a peaceful sporting event without boundaries, nothing more, nothing less.

before the Games, he lobbied in his regular worldwide press releases for the outright exclusion of "Negroes," referring to them as "black auxiliaries," and declaring in one statement, "I myself would never shake hands with one of them."

Negroes, of course, weren't the only race targeted by Adolf Hitler. It wasn't

until the International Olympic Committee threatened to pull the Games from Germany that he agreed to allow Jews on the German team, and to take down anti-Semite billboards leading to the Olympic city.

Hitler's agenda, then and later, was never subtle. His intent was to use the Olympics to certify his theories concerning the superiority of the blond-haired, blue-eyed Aryan race. To that end, he was determined that Aryans would produce, and dominate, the best organized, most spectacular Olympic Games ever. At that, Hitler did succeed in producing some of the most impressive innovations in Olympic history. It was the Berlin Games, for example, that introduced the torch relay direct from the sacred grove of Zeus in Olympia, Greece (the flame was carried into the Opening Ceremonies by none other than Greece's Spiridon Louis, winner of the first Olympic marathon in 1896); and it was the Berlin Games that first used live television and sent out press releases (propaganda) to news outlets around the world.

There were all kinds of little grand touches as well, such as every gold-medal winner receiving a year-old oak seedling as a "gift from the German people."

Had it not been for restraints of time, money, and war plans, Hitler would have gone even further. Among his schemes that didn't happen was a 400,000-seat stadium he wanted to build in Nuremberg, a stadium he envisioned as the permanent Olympic stadium "for all Games to come."

In the end, he had to content himself with the 120,000 jewel of a stadium built in Berlin, which was jammed to its limits every day.

In sharp contrast to Adolf Hitler's grand hopes and schemes, James Cleveland (Jesse) Owens came to Berlin with no other cause than running faster and jumping farther than anyone else. This son of sharecropping farmers and grandson of slaves was the very antithesis of militancy, an accomplished sportsman — he already held six world records — whose choice was to compete in peace.

That it was a time of considerable social upheaval is a given. It was common knowledge that Hitler almost lost the Games because of his racist views, and many disagreed that the Olympics should remain in his care. When plans for an "alternative" Games in Barcelona were thwarted by the Spanish Civil War, America almost pulled out completely. Only a 58-56 vote by the Amateur Athletic Union cleared the way for the U.S. team to go to Germany.

Even in Berlin, the feelings didn't still. In a concession to Hitler, the U.S. left Marty Glickman and Sam Stoller, the only two Jews on the team, off the 4x100 relay team, replacing them with Owens and Ralph Metcalfe.

Owens, not wanting to take the place of two runners who had long been training for their event, protested. "I've won enough medals," he said, having already won at 100 meters, 200 meters and the long jump. But when U.S. track coach Lawson Robertson said, "You'll do as you're told," Owens, the consummate team player, did just that, carrying the baton on the second leg as the U.S. won by nearly a second and a half and set a world record in the process.

By that stage of the Games, of course, Jesse Owens had already become the *wunderkind* of Berlin, cheered and hounded for his autograph wherever he went. He set an Olympic record in every event he entered, and, well beyond that, displayed a sportsmanship that won over the overflowing crowds. He smiled constantly and waved to the crowd, he encouraged his competitors, and, in what could not only be called the emotional high point of the Berlin Games but all the Olympic Games as well, after edging the handsome German long jump champion, Luz Long, for the gold medal, he and the blond-haired Aryan — in full view of the Fuhrer — walked off the field arm in arm.

In the space of a week in Berlin in 1936, it was Jesse Owens who redefined the Olympic Games as a peaceful sporting event without boundaries, nothing more, nothing less. It is the enduring legacy — and irony — of the Berlin Games that it was the "black auxiliary" from America, and not the dictator who tried to control them, who wound up winning over the world. ▼

BELOW / *Jesse Owens' legendary performance — gold medals in the 100, 200, 4x100-meter relay and the long jump — coupled with his genuine sportsmanship redefined the spirit of the 1936 Games in Berlin and overrode Hitler's attempt to turn the Games into a farce.* ALLSPORT

He is the only American to have won an Olympic Nordic skiing medal. Bill Koch claimed the silver in the 30-kilometer ski race behind Sergei Saveliev of the Soviet Union at Innsbruck in 1976. He competed in three more Olympic Games, in 1980 at Lake Placid, in 1984 at Sarajevo (pictured), and in 1992 at Albertville, where he launched a comeback to ski racing at the age of 36. ALLLSPORT/CANNON

The athletic Surya Bonaly of France finished fourth in the ladies' singles figure skating in Lillehammer. ALLSPORT/VANDYSTADT

What is a stretch of an imagination for most people is a gold-medal routine for Ekaterina Serebryanskaya of the Ukraine, who won the individual rhythmic gymnastics event in Atlanta. **ALLSPORT/RONDEAU**

THE WAITING GAME

Patience may be a virtue – but not necessarily when your sport of choice happens to be ski racing, where aggressiveness and tenths of seconds mean everything, and where careers, like missiles, tend to rise and fall in short bursts and quick gasps.

Which is why what happened to Gretchen Claudia Kunigk Fraser is so singularly remarkable. Not only did she become the first American alpine skier to win a gold medal in the Olympic Winter Games, but she did it after waiting out the cancellation of both the 1940 and 1944 Olympic Games and, finally, after waiting for the Swiss to fix their telephone line.

Hers was, to say the least, a lengthy run.

She first qualified for the United States Olympic Team prior to the 1940 Games, which were scheduled to be held, in order, at Garmisch-Partenkirchen, Germany; Sapporo, Japan; and St. Moritz, Switzerland, before they were canceled outright due to World War II. She was still on board to compete for the United States in the 1944 Winter Games, sched-

uled for Cortina d'Ampezzo, Italy, but that competition, too, was canceled on account of war.

By the time the 1948 Winter Games were awarded to St. Moritz, it was eight long years later, and now, instead of a promising ski racer barely out of her teens, Gretchen Fraser was nearly 29 years old.

> By the time the 1948 Winter Games were awarded to St. Moritz, it was eight long years later, and now, instead of a promising ski racer barely out of her teens, Gretchen Fraser was nearly 29 years old.

It would not have been unusual if she had dropped out in favor of younger competitors. The war caused many such casualties, including Gretchen's husband, Don Fraser, a member of the 1936 U.S. Olympic Ski Team and also a qualifier for the 1940 Winter Games – but who was

past his prime by the time the '48 Games came along.

But Don, remembering his pleasant Olympic experiences in Germany, urged Gretchen to forget her age and try out again for the U.S. team even if it had been six and seven years since she'd won her national championships in the downhill, the downhill-slalom combined, and the slalom. At the Olympic Trials, Gretchen competed against some girls nearly half her age – including a bright young 15-year-old named Andrea "Andy" Mead, who would go on to Olympic glory of her own four years later in Oslo – but, still, she held her own and finished as the No. 1 qualifier.

At St. Moritz she won her first medal six days before her 29th birthday in the alpine combined, a dual downhill-slalom competition that counted times from the official Olympic downhill along with times posted in a special combined slalom (in later years it would be termed the "giant slalom" and become an individual event). Gretchen was 11th in the downhill, but she finished a strong second in the slalom – enough to give her the combined silver medal between a pair of Austrians, Trude Beiser and bronze medalist Erika Mahringer.

To term her finish a "surprise" would be an understatement, given her age and the relative ineffective history of Americans, men or women, in international ski racing.

But the next day, in the Olympic slalom, the oldest member of the American team was back at it again, showing no strains of age or heritage, as she was assigned the difficult No. 1 starting position and nonetheless posted the fastest time of the first run. At 59.7, she was a tenth of a second ahead of Mahringer, four tenths up on Lucienne Schmit-Couttet of France, and a full second in front of the homeland favorite, Switzerland's Antoinette Meyer. If she could hang onto her lead she would win America's first alpine gold medal.

But first, it would turn out she'd need to exercise yet more patience.

This is how Alice Damarosch Kiaer, the manager of the U.S. women's team, set the scene in the official U.S. Olympic Committee report:

"We in the grandstands watched the girl racers slowly climbing up the long steep slope to the start in the beautiful setting of the Suvretta for that last ordeal to decide who would win the gold medal. There stood little Gretchen Fraser as the first racer ready to break the cord which started the timing. Then the unpredictable happened. The telephone from the top to the bottom failed ..."

Literally standing in the gate, ready to go, Gretchen was put on hold in the cold for 17 minutes as the Swiss frantically worked to repair the phone line.

As Kiaer continued in her report:

" ... and for seventeen minutes Gretchen stood there waiting for the signal to start. It was probably one of the greatest nerve strains to which a racer has ever been subjected."

The line finally repaired, Gretchen was off. Steeled, no doubt, by her eight years of waiting, she skied as if nothing had happened. She raced to an almost flawless second run that, as it turned out, would not be beaten by anyone other than Meyer, who used the urgings of the crowd to post the fastest time of the day and make up five tenths of a second on Gretchen. With her rally, Meyer was able to move into the silver-medal position, but still a half-second behind the American.

"Never was there a more popular victory than Gretchen Fraser's," continued Kiaer in her report (perhaps a bit hyperbolic, given the Swiss venue and Meyer's inspiring second run). "As we drove back in the open sleigh through the pine forest to St. Moritz the crowds cheered and followed the new champion. Flowers, gifts and telegrams were already pouring into our hotel."

Kiaer concluded her account with this: "I write this report with great pride and satisfaction because I have always believed that the happy temperament and good sportsmanship of American girls particularly suited them to be winners at this exacting and nerve-racking sport. I do not believe that a girl who is too high strung, too conscious of her rivals, or too jealous of her fame, can be a great champion skier. There must be an inner harmony in the spirit of a great racer. To my mind all our girls had this spirit and it was supremely demonstrated in Gretchen Fraser." ▼

TOP LEFT / The faces of Nigeria's 4x100 women's relay team light up as the scoreboard announces its bronze-medal finish in Barcelona. ALLSPORT/MARTIN

TOP RIGHT / U.S. long jumper Mike Powell prays before he leaps in Barcelona. ALLSPORT/CANNON

LEFT / After winning at 200 meters in Barcelona, American Gwen Torrence gets a congratulatory hug from a gracious Grace Jackson Small of Jamaica, who finished sixth. ALLSPORT/MEEHAN

ABOVE / Overcome with emotion, bronze medalist Ato Boldon of Trinidad is embraced by American Jon Drummond at the finish line of the 100 meters in Atlanta. ALLSPORT/VANDYSTADT

The 50-kilometer walk was held on a hot and humid August day in Atlanta. Andrzej Chylinski of the USA finds temporary relief in the coolness of a water-soaked sponge. **ALLSPORT/LEAH**

K a r o l y . T a k a c s

CARLOS & LEFTY

The story is part of Olympic lore, an oft-told favorite, revived every four years, at least, or whenever the subject of stupendous performances comes up. It takes place, allegedly, in London in 1948 just prior to the beginning of the rapid-fire pistol shooting competition. The defending world champion and world record-holder from Argentina, Carlos Diaz Valiente, sidles up alongside a Hungarian named Karoly Takacs. Valiente recognizes Takacs as a competitor from a decade ago, before the war, when Valiente was the South American champion and Takacs was a member of the Hungarian national team that won the 1938 European championship. The Argentinian knows that Takacs lost his right hand, his shooting hand, in an accident with a grenade while on training maneuvers with the Hungarian Army before World War II.

"My friend Karoly," says Valiente, casting a pitying glance at Takacs' missing hand. "What brings you here?"

"Hoping to learn something by watching you," says Takacs.

Then, in a scene Hollywood would do cartwheels for, Takacs shows up at the shooting venue the next day as a competitor, proudly wearing Hungary's team colors, and, to the astonishment of all, proceeds to obliterate Valiente's world record and relegate the world champion to the silver medal as he, Karoly Takacs, the one-armed man, wins the competition ...

... with his left hand.

At 28, Major Takacs was on maneuvers when he picked up a grenade he thought was dead. It wasn't.

The story's punch line comes as the Hungarian flag is being lowered from atop the flagpole. As they're leaving the top steps of the winner's rostrum, Valiente turns to Takacs, smiles, and says, "I think you have learned quite enough."

Alas, the story is apocryphal. There is no way Valiente couldn't have known ahead of time that Takacs was entered in the meet. By the time of the rapid-fire pistol finals, the Olympics were five days old and the shooters had already spent plenty of time together at the Opening Ceremonies and on the practice range.

Not only had news of Hungary's "one-armed man" had more than sufficient time to become common knowledge, but well before the Olympics began, Karoly had already placed high at a number of pre-Olympic competitions in Europe, including the Hungarian shooting trials.

The part about losing his right hand to a grenade, however, is true, as is the part about Karoly Takacs coming back to win Olympic gold – twice – with his left hand.

And that's unbelievable – and inspiring – enough.

Indeed, in the estimable roll call of courageous Olympic comebacks, it occupies a niche all its own, as untouchable as it is unprecedented. What Major Karoly Takacs did, no one had ever done before, and isn't likely to do again.

Neither war nor age nor cancellation of two consecutive Games nor loss of limb could dissuade this indomitable man from his appointed "rounds."

The incident that took his hand was a freak accident that occurred as Hungary prepared for war. At 28, Major Takacs was on maneuvers when he picked up a grenade he thought was dead. It wasn't. It exploded as he held it in his right hand. The lucky part was that they were able to save his life. But not his hand.

At the time, Karoly had only recently returned from the European shooting championships, where he helped Hungary to the team title. Although not a participant in the Olympic Games in Berlin in 1936, he had been considered a strong candidate to represent Hungary in the 1940 Games scheduled for Tokyo.

But then came the war – canceling the Tokyo Games – and then came the grenade, canceling Karoly's career as a competitive shooter.

Or so it seemed.

Exactly when Takacs began practicing with his left hand is unknown. By his own admission he trained in secret. In his memoirs, he recounts that after the amputation his only official public comment was, "Do not feel sorry for me – I will one day return."

When the 1944 Olympics, scheduled for London, were also canceled, it gave Takacs more time to get ready. Finally, by the time the Games reconvened in London in 1948, he was able to qualify as a member of the Hungarian team.

At the shooting competition, held at Bisley Camp outside of London, Takacs shot quickly to the forefront, tying for the lead after the first round with Leonard Ravilo of Finland at 286 points, one point in front of the Argentinian favorite, Valiente, and four points ahead of Torsten Ullman of Sweden, the bronze-medal winner in 1936.

In the second half, Takacs' hand was even steadier. He was nearly perfect with his fifteen shots – the first five fired at eight-second intervals, the second five at six-second intervals and the final five at four-second intervals. He scored 294 points out of a possible 300. His total score of 580 was ten points higher than Valiente's existing world record, and even though the Argentinian also, with a score of 571, exceeded that mark, it was far from enough. Sweden's Sven Lundquist won the bronze, surging ahead of a fading Ullman, who placed fourth, and the Finn Ravilo, who finished fifth.

At the Helsinki Games held four years later, Takacs returned to prove, at 42, that he was no one-time Olympic wonder. After an opening round of 287 he was only tied for fifth, with Valiente, both of them behind the leader, Huelet Benner, a

U.S. Army officer stationed in Panama who the year previous had broken Takacs 1948 world record with a score of 582. In the second round, however, Benner faded out of sight, finishing 34th, as Takacs again saved his best for last. He shot 292 for 579, just one point off his London total. A Hungarian teammate, Szilard Kun, finished second after a final round of 294 and Gheorghe Lichiardopol of Romania was third, one point ahead of Valiente, whose score of 577 was six better than his silver-medal effort in London.

"Lefty" Takacs hung around for one more

Olympic appearance, in Melbourne in 1956, where, at the age of 46, he still shot 575 and finished eighth. After that he holstered his weapon and retired. He had definitely learned enough. ▼

ABOVE / *Hungarian Karoly Takacs, who lost his shooting hand in World War II, blew away the world record and the reigning world champion, Carlos Valiente, to grab the gold in the rapid-fire pistol competition in 1948. "Lefty" Takacs came back four years later to successfully defend his Olympic title.* ALLSPORT

In a memorable bronze-medal shootout, Italy, the defending Olympic water polo champion, outlasted Hungary, 20-18, in the centennial waters of Atlanta. Spain beat Croatia for the gold. **ALLSPORT/FORSTER**

Walter . Davis

MAKING UP FOR LOST TIME

At first he had a sore throat and said he didn't feel like going to school. His mother thought he was faking. But at the end of the afternoon he was still in bed, and that wasn't like Buddy. He was an active kid, hardly the kind to keep up the ruse once school was out for the day. Four days later his legs and ankles began to swell. Two days after that he couldn't move them at all. In the hospital the official diagnosis was poliomyelitis. Polio for short. The word that sent chills around the world. This was 1939. Every year, thousands contracted the crippling disease, and doctors were essentially powerless, left helpless beyond keeping the victims as comfortable as possible while the virus ran its course.

Walter "Buddy" Davis, the last of five children born to the Arthur J. Davises of Nederland, Texas, sure wasn't faking it.

He wound up spending three weeks in the hospital, eventually losing the feeling in his right arm in addition to both of his legs. But then the escalation stopped, thankfully, and he was able to at least go home, released to the custody of his bedroom, where he lay for eight more weeks, able only to watch the neighborhood kids playing baseball in the lot across the street.

When he finally went back to school he had braces on both legs and his right arm and most of the time the older kids would carry him from class to class. But

> ## Four days later his legs and ankles began to swell. Two days after that he couldn't move them at all. In the hospital the official diagnosis was poliomyelitis. Polio for short.

he hung in there and eventually shucked first the braces, and then the crutches that followed. His heels suffered the most damage. For years he had to first stand up and walk on his tiptoes until his heels got some circulation. He ran constantly to develop his leg muscles – even if he did look like he might topple over on his face.

The doctors, of course, recommended against strenuous activity, but Buddy came out charging anyway, treating the lengthy layoff in the middle of his ninth year as too many recesses missed; a deficit that simply had to be made up. If it involved movement, it was for him. He even got into boxing until his mother made him quit.

His body, too, seemed to be impatient to make up for lost time. Buddy grew so fast once he got healthy the people in Nederland swore they could see it happening. He was 6-foot-4 and 150 pounds when he entered high school and 6-foot-8 and 200 pounds two years later as a senior.

It was at Texas A&M, where he entered in the fall of 1948 on a basketball scholarship, that Buddy became versed in the high jump. He originally signed to play baseball in the spring, when basketball was out of season, but the track coach, a retired army colonel named Frank Anderson, talked him into trying the high jump. Buddy had won the district championship at 6 feet even in high school, but he thought that was the modest end of it until Col. Anderson suggested that he abandon his scissors style in favor the straddle form. When he cleared 6-4 almost immediately, Buddy was hooked. By the next year, the colonel had him using the western roll and he was really off; he jumped 6-5 as a sophomore, 6-9 as a junior and 6-10 1/2 as a senior, breaking the American record of 6-9 3/4 set way back in 1935 by Cornelius Johnson.

Still, Buddy Davis wasn't known as a high jumper as much as a basketball player, where his impact was swift and sudden. He led the nation in fouls as a sophomore – not bad for a kid who once

couldn't get out of bed — and as A&M's leading scorer and rebounder, he led the school to its first Southwest Conference championship in 29 years in 1951. That same year, Walter "Buddy" Davis was named third-team All-American. His athletic future seemed destined to collide with a new league just formed called the National Basketball Association.

But then came the summer of '52, and suddenly Buddy Davis' "hobby" took center stage.

Since his 6-10 1/2 American-record jump had the good timing to come at the AAU national championships, which also doubled as the Olympic trials, he found himself bound for the Olympic city of Helsinki, Finland. The high jump finals came early, on the second day of the Games. In a field of 36 competitors from 24 nations — including representatives from the Soviet Union, entered for the first time since the Russian revolution — the kid who'd had polio wasn't head and shoulders above everybody else, it just

seemed like it. He won with a jump of 6-8 1/2, exactly his own height, and while it was two inches below his own personal best, it was still an Olympic record, breaking the 6-8 mark set by Cornelius Johnson in 1936. The silver medalist, Kenneth Wiesner of the U.S., finished an inch and a half behind, representing, at the time, the largest margin of victory in the high jump since the 1904 Games in St. Louis.

Davis came home not just an Olympic hero, but an inspiration to victims of adversity everywhere, especially polio victims.

A year after his gold medal, Dr. Jonas Salk introduced the polio vaccine that would effectively eradicate the dread disease from the face of the earth, and Buddy Davis, who dedicated himself following the Games to setting the world high jump record, did just that with a jump of 6-11 1/2 on June 27, 1953, in the AAU nationals at Dayton, Ohio. After that he was free to turn professional and return

to his first love, basketball. He joined the National Basketball Association in time for the 1953-54 season and his knack for winning championships continued. He was with the Philadelphia Warriors when they won the NBA championship in 1956 and he was with the St. Louis Hawks when they won the NBA championship in 1958, the last team to beat the Boston Celtics in the NBA finals in nine years. After five seasons, 325 professional games, 1,558 points (4.8 points-per-game average) and 1,397 rebounds (4.3 per-game average), Davis officially retired as an active athlete. He had a world record, two NBA championships rings, and a gold medal to show for it — and somewhere, a pair of leg braces, long since discarded. ▼

ABOVE / *American Walter "Buddy" Davis didn't even bother to take off his track suit to make his qualifying jump in the 1952 Olympic Games in Helsinki. No matter, Davis went on to win the high jump with a jump of 6-8 1/2, exactly his own height.*
ALLSPORT/HULTON DEUTSCH

Eye on the ball: Table tennis in Atlanta was ruled by China, which took the top two places in both the men's and women's singles and doubles events. **ALLSPORT/VANDYSTADT**

Eye on the target: Melissa Marlowe of the U.S. reaches for her target in Seoul, but the talented and much-talked about college gymnast came up short in the medal count. **ALLSPORT/STRICKLAND**

Agnes . Keleti

HUNGRY FOR GOLD

It was mid-November in 1956 when gymnast Agnes Keleti, along with the rest of the Hungarian Olympic Team, boarded a plane at the international airport outside Budapest bound for Melbourne, Australia. The Olympic officials gave her a round-trip ticket. They had no idea she would not be returning with them. But Agnes did.

She loved Hungary, the land of her birth. She considered Budapest, with the Danube River carving its way between the hills and plains that divided the city, among the world's most beautiful places. But in 1956 she was 35 years old and she had seen too much tyranny.

It was off the streets of Budapest that her father had been dragged by German troops at the start of World War II. Literally dragged, and then loaded onto a train bound for Auschwitz, the Polish concentration camp where he was one of the estimated three million Jews killed under orders of the dictator Hitler.

Thanks to the benevolence of a Swedish diplomat named Raoul Wallenberg, Agnes – who was born Agnes Klein – and her mother and sister were spared their

own rides on that train to Poland. Wallenberg hid the women in a Swedish "safe house" until they were able to obtain forged papers that identified them as Christians. Thus armed, Agnes crossed into France, a trip far more precarious than any four-inch balance beam she would ever traverse.

She returned at the end of the war, cheered by the defeat of Hitler, but now Hungary was in the domain of the

> **Thanks to the benevolence of a Swedish diplomat named Raoul Wallenberg, Agnes – who was born Agnes Klein – and her mother and sister were spared their own rides on that train to Poland.**

Soviets and that, she would discover, wouldn't exactly equate to freedom either. Just two weeks before the Olympic team was to fly to Australia, on Nov. 4, 1956, thousands of Hungarians protesting Soviet oppression had been gunned down by 200,000 troops dispatched from Moscow.

For Agnes Keleti, a certifiable Hungarian

athletic hero with nine straight all-around national gymnastics championships to her credit, it was the final straw. She had returned once. She would not return again. She arranged for her mother and sister to meet her in Australia, from where they would begin anew.

But first, she would wear the Hungarian colors one more time in international competition – her 24th such representation for her homeland. This would be her second Olympic Games. It might have been her third, if not for the injury two days before the London Games in 1948 that knocked her from the competition. The Hungarian team placed second that year, the last of team-only gymnastics competition for women. In 1952 in Helsinki, individual events were added, giving the women equal status with the men. The world was changing, and Agnes Keleti was there for the change. At 31, she won four medals in Helsinki, a bronze in the uneven bars, a bronze in the team exercise, a team silver in the combined competition, and a gold in her specialty, floor exercise. She finished sixth in the first-ever women's all-around, behind four Soviets. Despite a first in floor exercise, a third on the bars and a fourth on the beam, her medal hopes were dashed by a disastrous 41st place in her nemesis, the vault.

At the advanced gymnastics age of 35 – and just a month from 36 – Agnes was hardly the favorite coming into Melbourne. The Soviet team was, again, loaded – and with fresh new faces. The most vaunted of the new Soviets was a 21-year-old Ukranian, Larissa Latynina, a gymnast who would go on to win an unprecedented 18 Olympic medals in her career — nine of them gold.

But this was, after all, 1956, and the athletes from Hungary were nothing if not motivated. They couldn't get the Soviet troops off the streets of Budapest by what they did halfway around the world in Australia, but they could make a statement about the Hungarian spirit.

And make one they did. When the dust finally cleared in Melbourne, only the Soviet Union, the United States and the hosting Aussies had more overall medals and gold medals than Hungary, with nine golds and 26 medals overall.

Thirty-year-old Hungarian boxer Laszlo Papp first showed the way with an inspired victory over Jose Torres of the United States in the light middleweight division. It was Papp's third straight Olympic medal, and it came at the expense of a boxer who would go on to become the world light heavyweight professional champion.

The Hungarian water polo team took the cue from Papp, winning the gold medal with a 7-0 record that included a 4-0 shutout of the Soviet team. The match with the Soviets was marred by brawls and finally had to be stopped early by the Swedish referee, who feared a riot by the 5,500 spectators who were as anti-Soviet as they were pro-Hungarian.

It was onto this emotional stage that Agnes Keleti emerged. And while no punches were thrown as she dueled with Latynina and the rest of the Soviet team, there was plenty of the same kind of intensity. Agnes had never known better form. She won four gold medals, in floor exercise, beam, uneven bars and team exercise, a silver in team combined, and, finally, a silver to Latynina in the all-around. Despite first places in three of the four events, it was her 23rd place finish in the vault (won by Latynina) that again held her back.

Still, her total haul of six medals and four golds exceeded Latynina by one on both

counts, making Agnes Keleti, the one-time war refugee, the most decorated female gymnast in Olympic history in one Olympic Games.

Now she was a war defector. She participated in a six-week tour of the United States with 33 other defecting Hungarian athletes and four Romanians. She saw the White House, she met Louis Armstrong in Miami Beach, and she saw the Statue of Liberty and the Liberty Bell in between a series of gymnastics exhibitions. Once back in Australia she collected her mother and sister and they emi-

grated to Israel, where she was promptly hired as a gymnastics coach at a college in Tel Aviv. She married a year later, had two sons, and settled into a new life in her new home. ▾

ABOVE / *Hungarian Agnes Keleti won four gymnastics medals in Helsinki at the age of 31. Four years later in Melbourne, a month shy of her 36th birthday, Keleti won six more medals for an Olympic career total of five gold, three silver and two bronze medals.* SPORT MUSEUM OF FINLAND

Up against a field of seasoned skiers in Lillehammer, 16-year-old Italian Isolde Kostner collected two bronze medals in the downhill and the combined downhill. **ALLSPORT/VANDYSTADT**

L i s . H a r t e l

NEVER GIVE UP

There are certain things a horse just knows. A horse knows if its rider is scared or experienced. A horse knows when you sit astride its back whether you know what in the world you're doing up there. The way a rider flexes his, or her, thigh muscles, presses with his knees, sits up in the saddle and holds the reins, they mean a great deal to a horse. Do them poorly and the horse will barely move, or possibly throw you to the ground. Do them correctly and the horse will walk, trot, canter and gallop.

Do them expertly and the horse can make you a champion.

Growing up, Lis Hartel did all of these things as well as anyone in Denmark. As a girl she learned how to use her young legs not only to get her horse to obey her subtle commands, but to eagerly want to. It was a love affair between a girl and her horse, and later a woman and her horse. The result was national fame as one of Scandinavia's most accomplished riders.

Then one night in September of 1944,

with a two-year-old child to care for and another child on the way, it all came to a screeching halt. Lis was awakened by a stiff neck, and within a week her body was paralyzed with polio. Her world of canters and trots had suddenly become one of a full-time prone position in a hospital bed and a real concern not about whether she would ever ride a horse again, but whether she and her unborn child would even survive.

> Her legs were permanently paralyzed from the knees down and her thigh muscles were so weak there were almost no messages from the brain getting through. And the horse knew.

Fortunately, after four long months in the hospital, the baby was born normal and healthy, but the same would never again be said about the baby's mother. The doctors told Lis if she worked extremely hard she might be able one day to support herself on two canes, but that any realistic use of her legs would not be possible. Riding a horse again – that was out of the question.

Once home from the hospital, she set to work. With the aid of her husband and her mother, Lis began to try to develop the muscles of her arms and her legs. The announced objective – and it was doubtful – was to support herself on those two canes.

Only Lis knew her real goal was to ride her horse again.

That thought – to mount her horse's back and feel once again complete – drove her onward.

At first, the regimen was so painful it could only be pursued for minutes at a time. With a pulley above her bed, she strained mightily to achieve even the slightest movement of an arm or a leg. The day she could lift her arm was cause for a huge family celebration.

Next came the crawling, just a few inches at a time, progress so slow that many times she felt like giving up. But she kept at it day after day, month after month, until finally she supported her own weight on the two canes.

It was while sitting in her wheelchair one afternoon that she announced that she wanted to ride Gigolo, her old horse. To say everyone was stunned would be a gross understatement. It couldn't be done, they all said. But when this resolute Danish woman wouldn't back down, they took her to the stables and lifted her onto the horse's back. Just as they all suspected, Lis promptly fell off.

There was virtually no feeling in her lower limbs. Her legs were permanently paralyzed from the knees down and her thigh muscles were so weak there were almost no messages from the brain getting through. And the horse knew. The horse was smart, without a phony bone in his body. A human might fib a little, tell Lis she looked good up there, that she was riding really well, but not Gigolo. Gigolo knew, and so she fell, and fell again and again.

She gave up more than once. But always she would return, getting back on that horse with the help of her husband and mother, without whom she freely admits she would have had no chance to fulfill her dream.

Lis Hartel tried again, and again – until she was able to sit on Gigolo without falling off. And then the miracle began. She worked with her horse until all the things she *could* do – from her soothing voice to her balance to the weight shifts of the few muscles she could control – were able to compensate for all the things she *could not* do.

And she started riding, really riding, again.

Just three years after her polio attack she was able to enter regional meets in Scandinavia. The people who knew of her disease were astounded. She had to be helped into the saddle every time, but then she would ride just as well as any woman with two working legs.

Her skills continued to improve and in 1952 she entered the Helsinki Olympic Games. When she was lowered into the saddle for her turn the entire arena went quiet. As she took her horse from a trot to a canter and then a gallop it was as if she and her horse were one. He had the legs, she had the style. Together, competing against the top riders in the world, they won the silver medal.

When they hoisted the Danish flag up the flagpole, Lis Hartel could not hold back the tears. All those hours crawling on the floor, all those days hooked up to

the pulley in her bed, all those moments of despair and gloom, they were all worth it now.

Her polio would stay with her until her dying day. But so would her spirit and her drive. She again won the silver medal four years later – again in individual dressage – when the equestrian events of the 1956 Olympic Games were held in Stockholm. Again she was moved to tears, and again, the world cried with her.

Her Olympic performances served as a shining example to untold numbers of polio victims throughout the world. "Never give up" was her constant theme as she would correspond with large numbers of fellow polio sufferers. "Keep on trying to do better," she would urge, "you can do almost anything if you only believe it hard enough." ▼

ABOVE / Lis Hartel's love of horses and dream of the Olympic Games could not be subdued by even paralysis. The resolute Dane crawled her way back onto her old horse and eight years later won a silver medal in the individual dressage event in Helsinki and again in Stockholm four years later, where the equestrian events of the 1956 Melbourne Games were held. ALLSPORT

The Canadians won their first Olympic gold medal in the 4x100-meter relay, a team composed entirely of Jamaican-born sprinters. They relegated a well-beaten U.S. team to second place. Pictured, number three man Bruny Surin gets ready for the hand-off from Glenroy Gilbert. ALLSPORT/FORSTER

Part of the lure of gymnastics is how effortless the athletes make look what most people consider death-defying feats. **ALLSPORT/MARTIN**

Tommy Kono

NO LIMITS
(NOT EVEN THE SKY)

He was an anemic, sickly, emaciated little boy who suffered from chronic asthma from the age of two; the archetypal 90-pound weakling who got sand kicked in his face. On top of that, they put him in a prison camp of sorts during World War II when he, his three brothers and his parents, recent immigrants from Japan, were ushered out of their home in Sacramento, Calif., and herded into a Japanese-American detention camp in the mountains of northern California. "For your own protection," they told the Konos. In Tommy Kono's case, no one was arguing.

His given name was Tamio, but in an attempt to fit in, he soon switched to an Americanized version. He was 14 when he arrived at the Tule Lake Relocation Facility. He slept in a barracks and couldn't go to town on weekends because, well, there was no town.

But as well as cruel twists, fate can deal some kind ones, too. Two big breaks would soon reveal themselves amid the confinement and containment at Tule Lake – silver linings among the dark clouds of war. For starters, the high mountain air had a soothing affect on Tommy's asthma and other ailments. All of the traditional Japanese remedies tried by his mother – everything from powdered snakes to bear kidneys – hadn't worked, but the mountain environment did.

Something else that worked was when Ben Hara, an older neighbor kid from the next barracks, befriended Tommy and took him to the camp's workout gym.

He would look longingly at the posters around town advertising Charles Atlas bodybuilding correspondence courses. He wanted to look like the guys in the posters. He wanted to be strong and confident. He didn't want anybody kicking sand in his face.

A weightlifter was born.

As a younger boy growing up in Sacramento, Kono would recount later, he would look longingly at the posters around town advertising Charles Atlas bodybuilding correspondence courses. He wanted to look like the guys in the posters. He wanted to be strong and confident. He didn't want anybody kicking sand in his face. But he didn't have the money to send away for the course, and besides, he didn't think he was strong enough to lift the weights if he did.

But the trips to the Tule Lake gym changed that thinking. It was love at first barbell. He found that he could, as a matter of fact, lift the weights. Maybe not as many weights as his buddy could lift, but he could still lift them, and he could tell he was getting stronger as a result.

A year later, the war over, he returned to Sacramento with a completely changed mental outlook; he figured that if he, the original 90-pound weakling, could get healthy and strong, then anything's possible. The sky is not the limit. The only limit is what your mind tells you you cannot do.

What Tommy Kono did for the next decade of his life proved that over and over again. Once he started lifting weights, he never slowed down, or, more amazing yet, plateaued out – the plague of all lifters. Tamio Kono would not just set 41 international records and 26 world records from 1950 through 1960, he would not just go undefeated, during the height of his weightlifting career, for more than six years, but he would do all this and more while switching weight classes like he was getting on and off an elevator.

Of all the amazing accomplishments of this one-time asthmatic detention camp inmate, the most amazing is: He won three Olympic medals in three consecutive Olympic Games in *three different weight classes.*

He won a gold medal in Helsinki in 1952 as a 148-pound lightweight.

He won a gold medal in Melbourne in 1956 as a 181-pound light heavyweight.

And finally, as a 30-year-old in Rome in 1960, he won a silver medal as a 165-pound middleweight.

A lot of people thought he was more than one guy.

His method for adding or dropping weight was simple. If he needed to bulk up he would eat six to eight meals a day. If he needed to drop pounds, he would back off to a basic three.

It was his 33-pound, two-class jump from 1952 to 1956 that stamped Kono as an ultimate competitor. As a 22-year-old lightweight in '52, he'd set an Olympic record with his total of 797 1/2 lbs (362.5 kilograms) lifted in the three events of press, snatch and jerk (the jerk was eliminated from Olympic competition after the 1972 Games). Then, four years later as a bulked-up 26-year-old light heavyweight, 33 pounds heavier and that much stronger, he set a world record by lifting a grand total of 984 1/2 lbs (447.5 kilograms). Not only was his Melbourne total an astounding 187 lbs (85 kilograms) higher than his total as a lightweight in Helsinki, but to that point in Olympic weightlifting history only one lifter in *any* weight class — super heavyweight John Davis in 1952 — had amassed a higher total.

In what would be his final Games in Rome, Kono opted for the middleweight class just so he could get a shot at Aleksandr Kurynov, a vaunted new lifter from the Soviet Union. Their showdown

proved to be a riveting battle. Kono took the lead with an Olympic record press of 308 1/2 lbs (140 kilograms), after which Kurynov answered back with an Olympic record of 291 1/2 lbs (132.5 kilograms) in the snatch. They came into the final event, the jerk, tied for the lead, but while Kono managed a very good 352 lbs (160 kilograms), Kurynov lifted 374 1/2 (170), setting a world record and securing the gold medal in the process.

Both Kurynov's 962 1/2-lb (437.5-kilogram) total and Kono's 940 1/2 lbs (427.5 kilograms) were higher than any Olympic middleweight winner in history.

After that Tommy Kono retired, but only in a matter of speaking. He was named Mr. Universe as a bodybuilder in 1961, the third time he'd been given that dis-

tinction, and he became an Olympic coach in great demand. He served as the head coach for Mexico's weightlifting team in 1968, as West Germany's head weightlifting coach in 1972, and finally as the United States head weightlifting coach in 1976. In 1990, he was named to the United States Olympic Hall of Fame, the most decorated, prolific and versatile weightlifter in his country's history. ▼

ABOVE / *American Tommy Kono won a gold in Helsinki as a 148-pound lightweight (pictured). In Melbourne, four years later, the weightlifter, now 181 pounds, won the gold in the light heavyweight division. And in Rome, he slimmed down to 165 pounds to win the silver as a middleweight.*
SPORT MUSEUM OF FINLAND

In Atlanta, the pack, led by Japan's Yuko Arimori, keeps the leader Fatuma Roba within eyesight and what seems like striking distance, but the tireless Ethiopian outran them all for the gold in the marathon. Arimori faded to third place. **ALLSPORT/GARY M. PRIOR**

Hold that pose: U.S. gymnast Blaine Wilson hangs in midair in Atlanta. He wound up seventh on the rings. ALLSPORT/ M. POWELL

Irena Szewinska

SUPER WOMAN

Because of everything she accomplished over the course of a long and storied 16-year track career, the dozens of world and European championships, the multiple lowering of world records, the record seven track and field Olympic medals collected in a record five different events, it's easy to cruise right past Irena Szewinska's most remarkable accomplishment; namely: what she did when she had nothing left to prove.

The story begins in the Munich Games in 1972, where the 26-year-old Szewinska, long established as the first lady of the track, was obviously on her last, sore legs. A slightly sprained ankle caused her to pull out of the long jump competition before it even began, saving herself, she hoped, for her specialties, the 100 and the 200 meters, distances at which she'd set and reset numerous world records since splashing on the scene as a triple medal-winning 18-year-old in Tokyo in 1964.

But she flamed out royally in the 100, finishing a distant sixth, before salvaging a modicum – if that – of pride by placing a distant third in the 200. Finally, before clearing out of Germany for good, she

pulled herself and her lame ankle from Poland's 4x100 relay team.

It was inevitable, of course, that it had come to this; that the great Szewinska should finally be worn down, and out. That's what the sports columnists were writing back home in Warsaw, and, on paper at least, it made sense. Irena's had been a most glorious run – her third-place finish in the Munich 200 brought the sum of her medal haul in three

> The first time she ran an official 400-meter race she won the race in 52 seconds flat, just one second off the world record.

Olympics to a tidy two golds, two silvers and two bronzes – but not only was she now 26 years old, but an old 26 at that. Never one to concentrate solely on her running, Irena also managed to get an economics degree from Warsaw University, marry a sports photographer and one-time hurdler named Janusz Szewinska, and, in 1970, give birth to their son, Andrej. After all that, it was wonder enough, her critics contended, that she'd been able to come back in Munich and win one more medal, no matter what the color.

Certainly no one expected to see her in the Olympics again.

It was at this juncture that Irena

Kirszenstein Szewinska made them all think she'd lost her mind.

Not only did she choose NOT to retire, this new mother of a two-year-old also announced that she would hire her husband as her new coach. And she would add yet another event – the 400-meter run – to her repertoire of races.

Writing her memoirs would just have to wait.

Szewinska was bound and determined, it seemed obvious, to stomp on her storied past. Not only was she approaching old age – she'd be 30 at the next Olympics, which seemed an especially odd time to add the 400, an event generally considered the most grueling of all; but, on top of that, what was she doing hiring her husband, a man whose own modest athletic career was as a hurdler and who had never been a coach in his life?

Luckily for Irena, single-mindedness and a quiet independence had always been her long suit. She had been born in exile, in a refugee camp on the outskirts of Leningrad of the Soviet Union, where her Jewish parents had fled ahead of Hitler's invasion of Poland in World War II. Her family returned to Warsaw not long after Irena's birth. When she began school, her mother said, Irena never walked to the schoolhouse, but always ran.

It was that way, too, with her "comeback." The first time she ran an official 400-meter race – in September of 1973, a year following the disappointments of Munich – she won the race in 52 seconds flat, just one second off the world record. The second time she ran the 400, she knocked 1.1 seconds off the world record and clocked 49.9 – the first time in history a woman had broken the 50-

second barrier.

In the meantime, Irena had rebounded at the shorter distances as well. Throughout 1974 she was unbeaten at 100 meters – 23 races, 23 wins – and at 200 meters she not only won 19 of her 20 races but set another world record.

By the time the 1976 Olympic Games in Montreal were imminent, Janusz Szewinska was the smartest coach in Europe, and Irena was a genuine gold-medal favorite at whatever distance she chose to run.

Her preference going in was to try for a 200-400 double, but the schedule was not conducive so she settled on concentrating solely on the 400, the one distance at which she hadn't medaled. The 400 was extra appealing because of a phenomenal runner from East Germany, 18-year-old Christina Brehmer, who had just burst on the scene. In a race just two

months before the Olympics, Brehmer became the second woman in history to break the 50-second barrier when she eclipsed Irena's world record with 49.7.

A classic confrontation between the 18-year-old teenager and the 30-year-old veteran loomed.

The eagerly anticipated Szewinska-Brehmer showdown lived up to all expectations – for three-fourths of the race. Brehmer had the lead at the halfway point, and still held Irena at bay with a hundred meters remaining, when suddenly Szewinska blew past, not stopping until she broke the tape in 49.29 seconds, nearly half-a-second ahead of the world record and an amazing 10 meters in front of Brehmer.

Irena Szewinska, the oldest women's winner in Montreal, set a record by collecting a medal in four successive Olympics, she set another record with her seven medals

overall, and she set yet another record with her medals in five different events (most ever by a woman in Olympic track and field, and just one behind Paavo Nurmi's overall record of six).

A year later, in the 200-meter final of the first-ever World Cup, Irena defeated East Germany's Barbara Eckert, the winner of the Olympic 200 in Montreal – giving Szewinska her 200-400 double in an unofficial kind of way. She didn't wind up losing in the 400 until 1978, her string ending at 34 races and five years – five years when she wasn't even supposed to be running. ▼

ABOVE / Poland's Irena Szewinska, here outdueling Marita Koch in the 1977 World Cup, didn't get older, she just got more dominating. Her career wound up including five Olympic Games, five different events, and seven medals overall. ALLSPORT/DUFFY

The pressure ended up toppling the world champion and pre-Olympic favorite Kim Zmeskal of the United States, but she and her teammates rallied to a bronze-medal finish in the team competition in Barcelona.
ALLSPORT/MORTIMORE

Staying focused as you plunge from the three-meter springboard to the pool doesn't always mean you're as pretty as a picture.
ALLSPORT/BRUTY

Shun . Fujimoto

WHAT A MAN

Going into the 1976 Olympic Games in Montreal, Shun Fujimoto was hardly the best-known member of a strong Japanese men's gymnastics team intent on keeping alive a string of gold medals that extended all the way back to the Rome Games of 1960. The Japanese had their stars, including returning gold medalist Mitsuo Tsukahara and the great Sawao Kato, Olympic all-around champion in both 1968 and 1972, and they had their depth. Along with the other four members of the team, Fujimoto was part of the depth.

That depth was important, since the Japanese were braced for yet another showdown with the Soviet Union. It had become a regular rite of the Olympics. Every four years one of them would finish first and the other second. In 1952, the first year the Soviets began coming to the Games, and again in 1956, it was the USSR that won the gold and the Japanese the silver. In the four Games since, from Rome in 1960 through Munich in 1972, the Japanese had been able to reverse the trend – them first, the Soviets second.

No one expected the rivalry to abate in Montreal, and indeed, once the competition got underway, it became clear that it was business as usual. In no time, the Japanese and Soviet teams distanced themselves from the field, able to focus only on each other. As always, every hundredth of a point mattered.

> It was late in the competition that Fujimoto heard a crack in his left leg while executing his floor exercise routine. It sounded bad, and hurt worse. Fujimoto had shattered his knee cap.

It was late in the competition that Fujimoto heard a crack in his left leg while executing his floor exercise routine. It sounded bad, and hurt worse. He barely finished his routine and then immediately paid a visit to the team doctor, whose diagnosis was even worse than the pain. Fujimoto had shattered his knee cap.

Stunned, and with the pain getting worse by the minute, he asked the doctor for a painkiller so he could continue. But the doctor told him a painkiller was against the rules.

Fujimoto had a decision to make, and he made it quickly: He would continue anyway. In a competition where the top five scores are counted in each event, he did not want to reduce his team to just five performers, increasing the pressure on his teammates by eliminating their all-important margin for error. Neither did he want to tell his teammates of his condition.

Keeping the news to himself, he went ahead with his pommel horse routine, managing to dismount without drawing any undue attention. So far so good. After that he moved on to the rings. His shattered kneecap wouldn't interfere with the actual work on the rings themselves, which depended primarily on upper body strength, and after being helped up, Shun Fujimoto proceeded to deliver one of the best rings performances of his life.

But all the while he knew the time would come for the dismount, which called for a twisting somersault and a solid landing, with both feet, onto the floor some eight feet below. He knew he had to hold the landing for the necessary time, and he knew he had to depend on that worthless leg to hold him up long enough to get his points.

He did and it did.

Barely.

In an act of unmitigated courage, Fujimoto came down solidly on both legs with his arms raised, his left leg bending ever-so-slightly on impact. He wore just a

In 1996, a young female American gymnast named Kerri Strug would do her own version of a "Fujimoto" when she dismounted from a vault and landed solidly on a severely sprained ankle while her team was engaged in a fierce competition with Russia. Like Fujimoto, she carried on because her team needed her. Like Fujimoto, in the final analysis, her team could have gotten by without her heroic landing. Also like Fujimoto, she held her landing just long enough to please the judges before collapsing from the pain.

Unlike Fujimoto, however, Strug's injury was known beforehand. A sold-out arena and a worldwide television audience grimaced in pain right along with her as she came down hard on her injured left leg. And they thrilled as she was carried in the arms of Bela Karolyi, her coach, to the winner's rostrum. The photograph of that scene became The Photograph of the 1996 Olympic Games. Kerri Strug was on the cover of TIME. She was on the WHEATIES cereal box. She became a hero overnight, and deservedly so.

Perhaps, like the rest of the world, Kerri Strug had never heard of Shun Fujimoto. Notoriety had not been his lot. He had returned to Japan after Montreal with a gold medal in his hand and a brace on his leg and he pursued his personal life in the quiet anonymity that is the norm for most post-Games athletes. He was never on the cover of any magazines or cereal boxes – and when later asked if he would do it again, knowing how much it hurt, the self-effacing Japanese champion smiled and said simply, "No." ▼

LEFT / *A healthy Shun Fujimoto of Japan executes a move on the horizontal bar in an earlier competition before his ill-fated injury during the 1976 Olympic Games.*
ALLSPORT/MORLEY

hint of a wince mixed with a broad smile he flashed at the judges. Then, the performance ended, his leg collapsed under him like a piece of brittle bamboo.

The judges, unaware of the injury, gave him a 9.7 – the best rings score of his career. Shortly thereafter, the Olympic physician who examined Fujimoto's leg stated: "It is beyond my comprehension how he could land without collapsing in screams. What a man." Fujimoto later admitted, "The pain shot through me like a knife."

His secret out, and his leg shot, he was not permitted to continue. But his teammates took undeniable momentum from the courage of their fallen teammate as the heated battle with the Soviets raged on – ultimately coming down to Tsukahara's final performance on the horizontal bar. The Japanese star needed better than a 9.5 to win. He scored 9.9, and the Japanese once again took home the men's team gold medal, beating the USSR by four tenths of a point, the closest margin of victory ever.

Soccer, the world's most popular sport, is limited to 16 teams in the Olympic program and countries qualify in pre-Olympic tournaments. In Atlanta, women's soccer was added to the Olympic program and the U.S. gold-medal team wowed the capacity crowds. West Germany, (pictured scoring on a penalty), won the bronze in Seoul but like another soccer powerhouse, Brazil, it has never clinched the men's Olympic title.

ALLSPORT/CANNON

Ruthie Bolton, a first lieutenant in the Army Reserves, was one of many weapons in the American arsenal that led them to a gold-medal victory in Atlanta. In the final, she had 15 points, five assists and five steals. ALLSPORT/BELLO

All of five-feet, two-inch Katrina Powell packed plenty of power in her swings. She was the leading scorer for Australia's gold-medal winning team in Atlanta.

A m y . V a n . D y k e n

A
BREATH-
TAKING
FEAT

She couldn't swim the length of the pool until she was 12. She couldn't swim back again until she was 14, when her training partners were eight-year-olds. She couldn't even go nowhere fast. In high school, the other girls didn't want her on their relay teams. The doctors told her she could never be an athlete. If you had lined up all the teenage swimmers on the face of the earth in the late 1980s, Amy Van Dyken – a chronic asthmatic who never left home without her four inhalers – might have been the slowest.

No one would have given her a chance to win a single Olympic gold medal ... let alone one for each inhaler.

What Amy Van Dyken accomplished in the Atlanta Games of 1996 was enough to take your breath away. Finally, it was everyone else who was gasping.

The four gold medals she won at the Georgia Tech Aquatic Center – including individual golds in the 50-meter freestyle and 100-meter butterfly, plus relay golds in the 400-meter freestyle relay and 400-

meter medley relay – accounted for the biggest first-place haul by an American woman in a single Games in 100 years of Olympic history. At 23, she not only went where no American female superstar, swimmer or otherwise, had gone before, but, at that, she nearly added yet another medal when she posted a personal record in the 100-meter freestyle race while finishing fourth, one away from the victory stand.

That close-but-no-medal finish in the 100 freestyle was Amy's first race in Atlanta and certainly did not portend the total and complete Van Dyken domination that was about to come. Much the same as Amy's first 16 years of swimming produced nary a hint about the heights she would reach.

Back when she was "Little wimpy, asthmatic weakling Amy Van Dyken."

That's in her own words.

"I wasn't even supposed to be able to train," Van Dyken explained in the face of worldwide media attention as she became an "overnight sensation" in Atlanta. "Just being able to do a workout is something many doctors said couldn't be done. They said I wasn't supposed to be an athlete – I wasn't supposed to be able to do this."

She was born with a particularly unre-

lenting strain of asthma, her suffocating breathing attacks susceptible to all the igniters. Whereas many asthmatics might have their attacks induced by either allergies, infection, or exercise, Amy's could be induced by all three. On top of that, she was allergic to, as she put it, "everything that eats, sleeps, grows and breathes."

> "Just being able to do a workout is something many doctors said couldn't be done. They said I wasn't supposed to be an athlete – I wasn't supposed to be able to do this."

As a six-year-old she couldn't go on school field trips because of all the dangers – colds, pollen and all that walking – lurking along the way. Trips to the zoo, even if someone were to push her in a wheelchair, were taboo because of the animal hair.

As a frail youngster, Amy was only reluctantly pushed into the pool on the advice of some doctors – and they were in the minority – who thought that the exercise, while an enemy to the asthma, might, over time, prove to be an even stronger asset. If done with moderation, of course.

Daily she would trudge to the local swimming club her parents belonged to in the Denver suburbs. Years went by before she could swim *widths*, let alone lengths. She grew tall before she grew strong. She was not hard to spot. When she was grouped with those eight-year-olds at age 14, she was already 5-foot-11.

But slowly she not only found strength in

the water, but a competitiveness as well. No matter what the doctors said, Amy realized she didn't want to just be a swimmer, she wanted to be an athlete. She wanted to compete.

And so she did. In spite of the doctors. In spite of the inhalers. In spite of being a head taller than the eight-year-olds. In spite of going out for her high school swim team and overhearing her relay teammates say, "We could win this, except Amy's swimming anchor."

The asthma didn't give in easily, or completely. Even after being named the 1994 collegiate Swimmer of the Year by the NCAA, and even after she took up residency in Colorado Springs as part of the National Resident Team, she was still being occasionally rushed to the hospital with asthma attacks. She took every medication allowable under the rules of international swimming, but that only got her breathing to about 60 percent of normal. Sometimes it wasn't enough. When her lung capacity got beyond the

danger zone, Amy would have to stop swimming completely.

But sometimes it was enough.

In Atlanta, it was.

At 60 percent, she was the scourge of the pool. At 60 percent, the world chased her. After being overhauled in the opening 100-meter freestyle race by world record-holder Le Jingyi of China, Amy came right back two days later in the 400-meter freestyle relay to pace the team (also including Angel Martino, Catherine Fox and Jenny Thompson) to an Olympic record after recording a 53.91 split – the second fastest in history.

After that, it was all over but the smiling. Day after day, Van Dyken celebration photos carried front pages in newspapers around the world. No one smiled bigger. She smiled and threw her winner's flower bouquet after prevailing in the 100-meter butterfly – over China's Liu Limin and teammate Martino. She smiled again after swimming the anchor

freestyle leg and teaming with 14-year-old breaststroker Amanda Beard, 15-year-old backstroker Beth Botsford and the 29-year-old Martino, who swam the butterfly, to win gold in the medley relay. And she smiled even broader in her fifth and final event when she set a U.S. record of 24.87 in winning the 50-meter freestyle race ahead of her vanquisher just six days earlier – China's Jingyi.

When the waters finally cleared, the United States women's team had seven gold medals ... And the girl with the inhaler had four of them. ▼

ABOVE / *Five events and four gold medals later, asthmatic Amy Van Dyken became an overnight sensation in Atlanta both for her struggle to become a champion swimmer and her enthusiasm that punctuated each victory.* ALLSPORT/BELLO

K e r r i . S t r u g

PLEASE, LORD, HELP ME OUT HERE

The tide had turned. That much was for sure. Maybe nothing else was clear as Kerri Strug lay sprawled on her back in front of a sell-out crowd of 32,040 in the Georgia Dome, suddenly the world's loudest gymnastics arena, and another billion or so tuned in to television sets stretching from one St. Petersburg to the other. Maybe no one knew for sure who was going to win, or by how much. But what was clear was that momentum – big Mo – had definitely shifted sides.

Want drama with your Olympic venues? How about this? In women's team gymnastics – an event the Russians (and their allies when they were part of the former USSR) had never lost since they began coming to the Games in 1952 – the team from the United States was in the lead and in a position to stomp all over history ... but now, in the moment of truth, the Americans, as Strug was the latest to demonstrate, had suddenly taken a preference for the prone position.

All that remained for the Americans was a solid performance on the vault, and 40 years of Russian dominance would be history.

It was a sharp departure from form for the U.S. women. Through the first three events of the finals – uneven bars, balance beam and floor exercise – they had routinely nailed their routines while increasingly distancing themselves from the longtime dictators of the sport. Heading into their final event, the vault, their lead over the Russians was nearly a full point – .897 to be exact, the gym-

nastics equivalent of lapping a runner. A lead that had some of the Russian gymnasts in tears as they moved to their final event, floor exercise.

All that remained for the Americans was a solid performance on the vault, and 40 years of Russian dominance would be history.

But suddenly – and this is what ushered in the drama – the Americans looked human. After the first four U.S. vaults, their lead, for the first time, had begun to dissipate. Nothing to get excited about, but the fact was, they needed one more solid routine ...

... and they were having trouble standing upright.

It began with the fifth U.S. vaulter, Dominique Moceanu, who sprawled backward onto the mat after both of her vaults. Her best score was a 9.2. Since a team gets to drop the lowest of its six scores on each event, Moceanu's uncharacteristic lapse – she had scored nothing less than 9.8 in the first three events – didn't mean the end of the world, or the gold medal, either.

What it did mean was that the team's

sixth and final performer, Strug — the team's best vaulter and defending national vault champion, needed to land a good one.

But on her first vault, Strug rushed too, going out fast and landing flat on her back. Her score: 9.162.

Meanwhile, over on the floor exercise — which typically moves slower than the vault — the Russians were gaining ground. And with their best two competitors yet to go, it didn't require a math major to decipher what a Russian score in the 9.9 range could do next to a U.S. score in the 9.1 range. A couple of 9.9's and what had only moments before seemed inconceivable now seemed very conceivable.

The U.S. needed Strug's vault. It was that simple.

Except it wasn't. The fall on her landing had brought with it a loud pop in her left ankle. At first Strug, incredulous that she'd somehow missed a vault she hadn't missed all summer, ignored it. A gymnast is used to pops. But when she moved to stand up she knew her ankle was badly hurt.

Tears sprang to her eyes. What a time to sprain an ankle! She needed this vault, this one lousy vault she could do in her sleep. Something she *had* done in her sleep. She needed it for the team and she needed it for herself — so she could qualify into the individual all-around finals, something she'd heartbreakingly missed by a mere .0012 when she'd competed as a 14-year-old four years previous in Barcelona.

She looked up at her coach — the renowned Bela Karolyi, mentor of champions, of Nadia and Mary Lou and the rest. For a fleeting second she appealed to him for mercy. "I'm hurt," she said. "Do

we need my vault?" But the question was rhetorical and she knew it. Of course her vault was needed. Even if someone was clairvoyant enough to know how the Russians on the floor were going to finish, she needed her vault.

"Go on," encouraged Karolyi, reducing coaching to its most simple yet most necessary level. "You can do it."

After a quick prayer ("Please, Lord, help me out here"), she got up. The world was

now watching. She had 45 seconds to return to the top of the runway, another 30 seconds to complete her vault. Seventy-five seconds to end this nightmare.

She limped her way back

Amazingly, when she began her sprint the limp was gone.

So was the herky-jerky quickness of the first vault. This time she lifted into the air,

twisted at full height, turned again and somersaulted back to earth — landing solidly, both feet firmly planted on the ground.

It was only after she was sure the judges had seen what they needed that she pulled her left foot off the mat and, as the dumbstruck arena burst into cheers at her score of 9.712, scrunched up her face in pain.

The medics wanted to take her directly to the hospital, but Karolyi would have none of it, wrapping his latest champion in his arms and carrying her off her stretcher and straight into the arena. They arrived at the winner's rostrum just in time for the presentation of the gold medal, and the playing of the American national anthem.

Atlanta had its iconic moment as Kerri Strug stood at attention with her teammates, balancing on her right leg, her left leg already in a brace to the knee.

Later that night she got the word: Two torn ligaments. Take two crutches and the rest of the Games off. She dropped out of the all-around competition, bequeathing her spot, ironically, to Moceanu. ▼

ABOVE / *Be it on the balance beam, floor, uneven bars or vault, Kerri Strug showed the poise of an Olympic champion.*
ALLSPORT/DUFFY

OPPOSITE / *Safe in the arms of her coach, Bela Karolyi, Kerri Strug became the instant hero of the Atlanta Games when she vaulted on an injured leg, securing a gold-medal victory for the U.S. women and, at the same time, ruining her chances at any individual gymnastics medal.*
ALLSPORT/PENSINGER

The two-day Nordic combined event demands excellence in both ski jumping (90-meter hill) and cross-country skiing, a 15-kilometer race held on the second day. The number of points from the previous day's jumping determines the starting order in the race. In Lillehammer, Takanori Kano of Japan (pictured) finished second to Norway's Fred Borre Lundberg in the individual event, but the Japanese ran away with the gold in the team event, four minutes and 48.1 seconds ahead of Norway. ALLSPORT/COLE

STIRRING COMEBACKS

"It is not yet midday gentlemen.
The days of history are long.
Let us be patient
and remain confident."

– Pierre de Coubertin,
Speech given at
University of Lausanne, 1934

Every four years the Games themselves come back, encouraging the youth of the world to do the same. Some take the call literal, producing, as a consequence, terrific tales of tenacity and determination – with a little plain stubbornness often thrown in for good measure. Breaking the tape is one thing, but breaking the tape after making up ground, after coming from behind ... now *that's* a story.

Some comebacks occur during the competition itself. Others begin long before the starter's gun ever goes off. Some comebacks are accomplished in less than a minute. Others in more than a decade. It took Launi Meili, Dan O'Brien, Michael Johnson, Mark Spitz and Phil Mahre four years – one long Olympiad each – to come back; it took Dan Jansen twice that; and Albert Hill had to wait out an entire World War. Joe Frazier's comeback, on the other hand, involved a ride on a relatively short wave of opportunity that swelled and fell in a little more than a week in Tokyo in 1964; and Jim Craig and the 1980 U.S. hockey team used roughly that same amount of time to completely reverse their fortunes vis-à-vis the mighty Soviets in Lake Placid.

Other comebacks are more symbolic – Peggy Fleming towing United States figure skating back from the tragedy of a plane crash that wiped out the entire "A" team; Valerie Brisco coming back from motherhood and the neighborhood; Teresa Edwards leading the resurrection of U.S. women's basketball; and, first but not least, pint-sized Spiridon Louis, a mailman and a shepherd in his day jobs, hauling the entire modern Olympic movement into the stadium in Athens in 1896 after finally overcoming the fast-starters from Australia, France, and the United States.

Comebacks. Equal parts patience and impatience; discipline and desperation. Always with thrilling endings to die for. Well, almost. ▼

Barcelona's now famous diving well at the Piscina de Montjuic with its dramatic backdrop of the city and the landmark spires of the Familia Sagrada made for a picture-perfect competition.
ALLSPORT/MARTIN

Spiridon Louis

THE STUFF OF LEGENDS

He was, by all the usual measurements, an ordinary man. He stood about 5-foot-7, weighed maybe 120 after a robust lunch of lamb and feta cheese; at 24, he had already taken his turn in the Greek army, married, and started a family in the country village of Maroussi, which explained his two jobs, as a farmer and a postal carrier. Spiridon Louis, a Greek peasant making his way as the nineteenth century was giving way to the twentieth, very much blended in with the landscape. No one had ever heaped gifts upon him, or tried to buy him dinner.

But all that changed on the afternoon of April 10, 1896, when Spiridon Louis, the mailman from Maroussi, entered the Pan-Hellenic Stadium in Athens after running 40 kilometers from the plains of Marathon faster than anyone else ...

... The afternoon he heard the shouts of a hundred thousand countrymen, the afternoon he rode on the shoulders of princes ...

... The afternoon he saved the modern Olympic movement and presented to the world an entirely new running event.

His fortuitous entrance came squarely in the middle of the first Olympics of the modern era. The sporting movement that would, in time, command the attention of every nation on earth, was teetering on the brink at the close of Day Five. The Greeks, who were hosting — and paying for — the modern re-entrance

A barber gave him free daily shaves for life. A shoemaker gave him free shoes for life. A haberdasher gave him underwear and socks for life.

of what was, after all, their invention, weren't getting much of a return on their investment. They had managed to win the occasional fencing and gymnastics event and a Greek had won in pistol shooting, but that was hardly compensation for what was — or was not — happening in the stadium, site of the signature track and field events.

By the time of the final track event — the distance run from Marathon — Greece was 0 for the Olympics.

It had been another long day in the marble-encased stadium, filled daily by upwards of a hundred thousand spectators. In the 100 meters, the high jump and hurdles, more Americans won, and in the pole vault, the Greek national champion placed a full foot and a half behind two Americans.

The partisan crowd grew irritable. For five long days now, they'd flocked to the stadium, passionate about the revival of their legacy. No pomp, pageantry or expense had been spared. Winners' heads would be adorned — by King George himself — with olive branches from the sacred grove in Olympia. But as the wreaths kept being claimed by "outsiders," it became harder and harder to hold a brave face.

The only hope left was in a distance race that, while the brainstorm of a Frenchman, hearkened to the very roots of Greek courage. The Frenchman, a historian named Michel Breal, was familiar with the story of Pheidippides, a Greek soldier who, in 490 A.D., had been dispatched to Athens to deliver news of victory following a battle on the plains of Marathon between the Athenians and the Persians. Pheidippides, as legend has it, ran the entire 40 kilometers, burst into the legislature, announced, "Rejoice! We conquer!" and then fell dead.

The Greeks were nothing if not enthusiastic about the re-creation. Runners throughout the country went into training, Spiridon Louis among them. In a final "trial" race held on the Olympic course a month before the Games, he qualified by finishing fifth.

On the day of the race, 17 runners from five nations converged in Marathon, including 13 Greeks, a Hungarian, and the first three finishers from the 1,500-meter race held three days earlier – Edwin Flack from Australia, Arthur Blake from the United States and Albin Lermusiaux from France.

Lermusiaux and Flack sprinted to an early lead, with Blake not far behind, and, as old women prayed in churches along the route that the winner might be a Greek, word filtered into the stadium that a Frenchman was winning. The crowd fell into a nervous funk.

But the notion of distance pacing was hardly familiar to the 1,500-meter runners. Soon Blake collapsed, and then, at the course's first significant hill, Lermusiaux dropped to the ground. Flack took the lead, but the Australian, too, with the packed stadium still seven cruel kilometers away, began to lose his rhythm.

It was then that the methodical Louis made his move. He passed Flack at 33 kilometers and, four kilometers later, moved out of sight.

About this time, a horse and rider entered the stadium and told the king that a Greek had taken the lead. The news spread like a gunshot. "A Greek!" "A Greek!" echoed off the marble walls.

When Louis, sunburned and sweat-drenched – but gloriously all alone – entered the stadium, the crowd was already on its feet, whipped to a frenzy. As Burton Holmes, an American travel writer, would later write, "Never has such a sight been witnessed since the

days of antique Athens."

On the final straightaway, Constantine, the Crown Prince, and his brother, Prince George, ran stride for stride with the peasant from Maroussi. At the royal box, King George threw his visor high as the princes, Constantine, George and Nicholas, hoisted Louis on their shoulders.

From the crowd, a woman handed Louis a pearl-adorned watch. Other gifts followed. A barber gave him free daily

shaves for life. A shoemaker gave him free shoes for life. A haberdasher gave him underwear and socks for life. An innkeeper gave him 365 free meals. He got a lifetime pass to the theater, and, in addition to the olive wreath, the king added a gold watch. One of the more unusual expressions of gratitude came from a Greek woman who offered a choice between a sum of money or a kiss. As Holmes described it, "Louis, with a spirit of an amateur, refused the lucre, and with the gallantry of an *Olympianiké*, accepted the other proposition."

After that, the marathon man assumed his old life. Spiridon Louis never ran another marathon or competed in another Olympics, getting out of the way of what he got started. The Boston Marathon began the next year in America, on Patriot's Day, and hasn't quit since, and there's no denying that the Olympics, once Louis entered that stadium, resumed their magnificent comeback. The Greeks got what they prayed for. Spiridon Louis did a Pheidippides all right, bursting into Athens as if to say, "Rejoice! We conquer!" — and then effectively fading into legend. ▼

ABOVE / *Spiridon Louis, the mailman from Maroussi, delivered the first and only track and field gold for his home country hosting the first Modern Olympic Games in 1896. Athens, hungry for a victory in track and field, received its marathon champion with gifts of gratitude.* ALLSPORT

Twenty-six-year-old Diann Roffe-Steinrotter staged the comeback of her ski career when she drew the number one slot on the super G course and then watched 56 skiers all come down slower. After winning a silver in the giant slalom in Albertville, the American suffered through two disappointing seasons on the World Cup. The gold in Lillehammer capped a career that began when she won the giant slalom at the World Championships in 1985 as a 17 year old. **ALLSPORT/M. POWELL**

Jean Luc Brassard of Canada upset France's Edgar Grospiron, the defending Olympic champion, to take the men's mogul title in Lillehammer. **ALLSPORT/COLE**

After testing positive for an illegal substance, Canadian Ben Johnson (right) was stripped of his 100-meter world record and gold medal in Seoul, which was awarded to American Carl Lewis (middle). This would be Lewis' last medal in the 100 meters. Linford Christie (left), who then won the silver, went on to clinch the Olympic title in Barcelona. The 36-year-old (and grandfather) Christie made it as far as the starting blocks at the 100-meter final in Atlanta, where he was disqualified after two false starts. ALLSPORT/PATRONITE

Evelyn Ashford (foreground), the 100-meter sprint champion in Los Angeles, took back seat to Florence Griffith Joyner in Seoul, who beat Ashford 10.54 to 10.83 seconds. ALLSPORT/PATRONITE

Wilma Rudolph

GO GIRL!

She came into the world two months premature, the 20th of 22 children born to poor black parents in Bethlehem, a segregated farm town in northern Tennessee. At four she contracted pneumonia, which was soon trumped by scarlet fever, resulting in a left leg twisted and bent to the point that it had to be placed in a brace. She was black, female, dirt poor, and crippled. If you had lined up the four billion or so people alive in the 1940s and calculated their odds at winning an Olympic gold medal in running, there wouldn't have been many any lower than Wilma Ruldoph's.

She never did see a doctor in Bethlehem, or in Clarksville either, the nearby city the Rudolph family moved to in her childhood. Wilma's mother, Blanche, would take her daughter once a week on the 90-mile round trip to Nashville to see the doctors there at the free clinic, who did the best they could for the rail-thin girl with the bent leg and chronically sore feet. They kept her in the brace for two years. Then they fitted her with an orthopedic shoe.

Things finally started to look up one day when she was 11 and took off the fitted shoe herself because of how badly she wanted to play basketball with her brothers. To her great relief – not to mention the great relief of her brothers, who had for years taken their turns massaging her leg – the leg could handle her weight, if only just. It was enough for her. Wilma Rudolph had been standing on the sidelines long enough.

Playing basketball on the dirt was one thing, of course. Getting beyond the borders of the black half of Clarksville was yet another. Segregation was still legal in

She was black, female, dirt poor, and crippled.

America, carrying with it its own set of challenges; and, too, athletic participation by females was hardly the norm in the '40s. There had been a few breakthroughs, notably by Mildred "Babe" Didrikson at the 1932 Olympic Games in Los Angeles, but for the most part American women lagged behind. As late as 1960, there hadn't been a world record set by an American woman runner in more than a quarter of a century, and no American woman had won a gold medal in the Olympic Games since Helen Stephens at 100 meters in 1936.

Such were the obstacles in front of Wilma Rudolph even after she could run under her own power.

She had two things going for her, however. One was her persistence; the other

was the fortunate placement of her birth. As it turned out, she couldn't have chosen a better place in America to be born. With Clarksville less than an hour's drive from Nashville, that made certain that Wilma, as she developed into a star basketball player and track standout at Clarksville's all-black Burt High School, caught the attention of Ed Temple, the head track coach at Nashville's Tennessee State University. At Tennessee State, Temple was quickly developing the premiere women's collegiate track program in the country, a program that would supply the U.S. with a majority of its women's track and field qualifiers in Helsinki in 1952, in Melbourne in 1956 and in Rome in 1960.

Temple began working with Wilma in her sophomore year of high school, making her a member of his summertime "Tigerbelles" when she was just 15. Within a year he'd already coached the 5-foot-11, 89-pounder into a sprinter to be reckoned with. At the U.S. Olympic Trials in the summer of 1956, the irrepressible 16-year-old came out of nowhere to tie 22-year-old Mae Faggs, her mentor and Tigerbelle teammate, in the 200-meter final. Just like that, Wilma Rudolph was an Olympian, qualifying for the 1956 Olympic Games in Melbourne.

No American women wound up winning individual medals in Melbourne even though both Faggs and Wilma ran times below the existing American record in the 200. The U.S. team in the 4x100 relay found a measure of redemption, however, when an all-Tigerbelles team that included Margaret Matthews, Isabelle Daniels, Faggs and Rudolph finished third, just four tenths of a second behind the host Australians.

Considering where she'd come from, that feat in and of itself represented a considerable accomplishment for Wilma Rudolph, who got back to Clarksville just in time to show off her bronze medal and lead Burt High School to the state basketball championship.

And indeed, it appeared Melbourne would be the start and finish of Wilma's Olympic adventure when she learned at the beginning of her senior year of high school that she was pregnant.

She dropped out of sports, although not out of high school, and had the baby, a daughter named Yolanda. She didn't marry the baby's father, Robert Eldridge, although she would five years later, after she'd "grown up." But at 17 she was able, once again, to turn to her family, and her coach, for support. One of Wilma's older sisters agreed to look after the baby and allow Wilma to accept an athletic scholarship to Tennessee State, where Coach

Temple agreed to waive his "no mothers" rule and let her on the track team if Wilma would commit to earning her degree.

Two years later, Wilma again qualified for the Olympic Games, this time at 100 meters, 200 meters and the 4x100 relay. It was at the 1960 Games in Rome that she successfully merged her name with Olympic lore. In the space of six days, she became the first American woman to win three gold medals in one Games as she set Olympic records in both of her individual races as well as a world record in the relay, where the American team again consisted completely of Temple's Tigerbelles.

After that she was the toast of the track world; she toured Europe, then the United States, then Africa; she made an appearance on the *Ed Sullivan Show*, she graduated from Tennessee State, and she set a half-dozen more world records

before retiring in 1962, at the age of 22, so she could marry Robert Eldridge, raise her daughter, go to work as a second grade teacher, and get involved in the civil rights movement.

Once she got started, Wilma Rudolph never did slow down. ▼

ABOVE / *A polio victim as a child, twenty-year-old Wilma Rudolph broke the tape in a wind-aided 11 seconds, winning the 100 meters in Rome. She also won the gold in the 200 meters and anchored the American 4x100 relay team for her third gold. It was the fourth consecutive time since the introduction of the women's 200 meters in 1948 that the same woman won both Olympic sprint events.* ALLSPORT

Imagine racing hard for several kilometers, stopping and stilling a slamming heart to steady a 22-caliber rifle and squeeze off five shots, the target 50 meters away. Race hard and repeat, three more times. This is biathlon. A miss in the men's 20-kilometer and the women's 15-kilometer races costs a minute; in the shorter races and the relays, a miss costs one lap on the penalty loop. Women's biathlon joined the Olympic Winter program in Albertville, pictured here. **ALLSPORT/VANDYSTADT**

Peggy　Fleming

ON HER OWN

On the day after Valentine's Day, 1961, one of the greatest disasters in American sporting history occurred when a plane carrying virtually every top figure skater and figure skating coach in the country crashed in Brussels, Belgium, en route to the world championships in Prague, killing all 73 on board, including 34 coaches, skaters, officials and family members.

Peggy Fleming was 12 years old at the time – safe at home in Pasadena, California.

Another a year or two older, and she'd have been on that plane.

But in 1961 she was still a novice – a *championship* novice, it's true, with a win in the 1961 Pacific Coast Championship's novice ladies division already to her credit earlier that fateful winter – but still, a pre-teen novice. Billy Kipp, her coach for the past three years – practically from the time she first put on a pair of skates – was taking care to bring her along slowly, surely, and soundly. Or at least that had been their plan ... until the plane went down. With Billy Kipp on board.

It was roundly believed that American figure skating at the elite level would not recover for a good long time after the Brussels' air disaster. Before the crash, the United States, with a succession of men's Olympic singles champions dating back through every Winter Games since 1948 and with women Olympic singles champions Tenley Albright and Carol Heiss wowing the crowds in 1956 in Cortina and 1960 in Squaw Valley, respectively, was undisputably No. 1, the world leader in figure skating. But all that changed with the tragedy. Even promising newcomers left behind, such as Fleming, were suddenly without coaching support.

> It was roundly believed that American figure skating at the elite level would not recover for a good long time after the Brussels' air disaster.

But if the heart and soul had been yanked out of the team, that was hardly the case with Peggy. Even as she mourned the incredible loss, the saddened and suddenly coach-less 12-year-old resolved to do everything she could to ensure that Billy Kipp's efforts wouldn't go for naught.

Luckily, her parents shared her resolve.

The Flemings weren't wealthy. Albert Fleming, Peggy's father, was a linotype operator. Her mother, Doris, was a homemaker. But as soon as it became obvious that their daughter had a natural affinity for ice skating – her first time on the ice, when she was nine and the family lived in Cleveland, she didn't so much as wobble – her goals *and* her expenses became theirs, and vice versa. Albert Fleming took a second job and Doris Fleming made Peggy's elaborate competition costumes – and each morning they pushed her out the door before dawn to get to the rink and practice. They were all determined that she'd make it.

After the plane crash, the Flemings wasted no time in securing the services of another coach, Carlo Fassi, a former Italian men's champion who had come to America thinking he might be able to help fill the coaching void left by the plane crash. Fassi and Fleming clicked from the start, and Peggy barely missed a figure eight. By 1963 she and her new coach found themselves at the national championships – they were held that year, coincidentally, on the same Cleveland Arena rink where Peggy first laced on skates six years earlier. As fate would have it, she won the ladies' title; at 15, the youngest national champion ever.

At the 1964 Olympic Winter Games in Innsbruck, United States skating, as predicted, did experience a downturn. For the first time since World War II, no

Americans won gold medals and just one, men's singles bronze medalist Scott Allen, won a medal, period. But in the women's competition the sixth-place finisher, 15-year-old Peggy Fleming, still managed to turn a few heads. It was obvious, she was just getting started.

Four years and four more U.S. national championships later, the Olympics convened in Grenoble and that 15-year-old was now a 19-year-old. This time, she turned a lot of heads, including those of all nine judges, who were so impressed by her technical ability in the opening compulsory figures competition they rewarded her with a 77.2-point lead going into the free skating portion of the program. English translation: she could have skated half of that program on her head and still won. At that, she gave it a try. Her free skating final program, skated in Grenoble's ornate *Stade de Glace* and choreographed to Tchaikovsky's *Pathetique*, was both daring and

innovative, incorporating a number of difficult jumps and sequences, including the first spread eagle-double axel-spread eagle combination ever tried by a woman in competition. The result was enough uncharacteristic slipping and falling that Peggy, dressed in her mother's best gown, burst into tears when the program was over. It was not her best night. Not that it needed to be. She actually increased her lead in the free skate and won by a huge margin – giving the United States its only gold medal in Grenoble.

With a decade of training and traveling debts to take care of, Peggy turned professional not long after the Olympics. The spoils came quickly and plentifully as she quickly accepted a half-million-dollar commentating deal from NBC as well as numerous offers to tour with the Ice Follies and star in television specials.

Her coronation as the first lady of American figure skating not only paid tribute to the more than 20,000 hours

she'd practiced during her 10-year amateur career and to the sacrifices of her parents, but to the coaches who showed her the way – both Carlo Fassi, who stayed by her side through two Olympic Winter Games (and who would go on to coach Dorothy Hamill to the women's singles gold medal in 1976), and, of course, the late Billy Kipp, who got her started.

Peggy Fleming indeed made good on her goal to make her first coach's memory proud. Thanks to her, instead of the world wondering what happened to American figure skating after the crash, few even realized it missed a beat. ▼

ABOVE / *Peggy Fleming gave the U.S. its only gold medal in Grenoble when she won the ladies' figure skating title.* ALLSPORT/USOC

109

In a field representing 44 countries, American Mike Gebhardt, who won the bronze in Seoul, captured the silver medal in the men's windsurfer class in Barcelona.
ALLSPORT/BILOW

OPPOSITE / Lillehammer marked the medal debut for aerials, a discipline of freestyle skiing that had been a demonstration sport at both the Calgary and Albertville Games. Andreas Schoenbaechler of Switzerland won the men's gold medal, while world champion Lina Tcherjazova of Uzbekistan collected the gold in the women's event.
ALLSPORT/BILOW

J o e . F r a z i e r

THE PUNCH LINE

In 1964 a promising 20-year-old boxer named Joe Frazier tried out for the United States Olympic Boxing Team. He had a wife and three children and a $100 a week job at Cross Brothers Slaughterhouse in Philadelphia. Frankly, he was barely getting by.

He was a good boxer, he knew that, but there were a lot of good boxers, and being regional Golden Gloves champion didn't exactly bring home a paycheck. He knew how much these tryouts could mean to his future. He had seen what Olympic success had done for Floyd Patterson, and most recently for Cassius Clay, the star of the most recent Olympic Games held in Rome, Italy. This was his big opportunity and he knew it, a chance to trade a meat cleaver for a boxing glove, a chance to make his mother and father proud of him back in Beaufort, South Carolina.

This was Joe Frazier's chance to turn a hobby into a well-paying career.

Then he didn't make the team.

He breezed through the preliminary rounds at the Olympic Trials, hardly working up a sweat as he powered his way to the championship round. But in the heavyweight final he was stopped by a 300-pound behemoth named Buster Mathis. It was a close fight and the decision could have gone either way. But it went 3-2 for Mathis and that meant all the difference. It was on to Tokyo for Buster Mathis and back to the slaughterhouse for Joe Frazier and his Olympic hopes of glory and grandeur.

Frazier's dream appeared dead, and indeed it would have died, then and there, had it not been for the fortuitous intrusion of Pat Duffy, the boxing chairman of the Middle Atlantic AAU and a true believer in Frazier's ability. Duffy urged Frazier to make the trip to Tokyo anyway. He told him he could go as a team alternate, a stand-in ready to fight if someone got hurt. Duffy even speculated that Frazier could box as a middleweight if he had to, a wild thought to be sure, given Frazier's 200 pounds.

But a faint hope is better than no hope at all, and it was on that basis that Joe Frazier acted on Duffy's suggestion. In October of 1964, with the Tokyo Games no more than a week away, he arranged for his own passport and expenses and packed his bags for the Orient – where he would be available just in case the U.S. team still needed him.

He flew first to San Francisco where Duffy had arranged for a short exhibition sparring bout between Frazier and Mathis at Hamilton Air Force Base. It was there that fate intervened. Mathis broke his left wrist during the exhibition and had the hand promptly placed in a cast. No one had to look far for his replacement. Suddenly, Joe Frazier was America's Olympic heavyweight contender, and Uncle Sam took over his expenses.

It was a rejuvenated Frazier who blazed through the preliminary rounds in Tokyo. He beat his first opponent, Australia's Arthol McQueen, so convincingly that the bout was stopped not long after it began. In the semifinals, he squared off against the Soviet Union's Vadim Yemelyanov – a big favorite to make the finals – and caught him with a crushing left hook at the two-minute mark of the second round. The blow was so devastating that the fight, too, was stopped early. That was the good news. The bad news was that the blow was so devastating it also broke Frazier's thumb. Later, he described how he heard, and felt, the snap and the searing pain in his hand just as he threw the hook.

Now here he was, staring at the heavyweight Olympic final in less than 24 hours ... and he had a broken thumb at the end of his left arm.

> ## This was Joe Frazier's chance to turn a hobby into a well-paying career. Then he didn't make the team.

He didn't tell anyone about it. He had seen what happened to Buster Mathis because of a broken wrist in San Francisco. He refused x-rays, even though others could see he was in obvious pain. He said he was fine. No problem. One way or another, he would fight for the gold medal.

He wound up fighting more like a middleweight – inadvertently proving Duffy, at least partially, a prophet – in the gold-medal bout against Germany's huge Hans Huber, a bus driver by profession. In the manner of lighter, more fluid, fighters, Frazier constantly plodded forward, moving and jabbing and punching relentlessly with his good right hand and doing his best with his left to block and jab and stab.

The strategy worked. Although the taller German outweighed and outreached the American, Frazier kept Huber, who was oblivious to Frazier's handicap, on the defensive from the opening bell.

Three rounds and plenty of feinting later, the judges declared the man with the undisclosed broken thumb the winner. "Smokin'" Joe Frazier walked away from the Korakuen Ice Palace as the Olympic gold medalist. He would never again pull a shift at the meat plant.

The rest of the Joe Frazier story, of course, is even better documented. "Smokin' Joe" would go on to become the undisputed heavyweight champion of the world, beating one Buster Mathis for the title in 1968. He would fight Muhammad Ali three times in the most memorable trilogy in the history of boxing. He would open his own boxing gym in Philadelphia where he would develop several Olympians. He would be inducted into the boxing Hall of Fame ...

...And all because, as a 20-year-old working in a Philadelphia slaughterhouse, he had the faith, and the courage, to head out for Tokyo as an alternate who might not even get to throw a punch. ▼

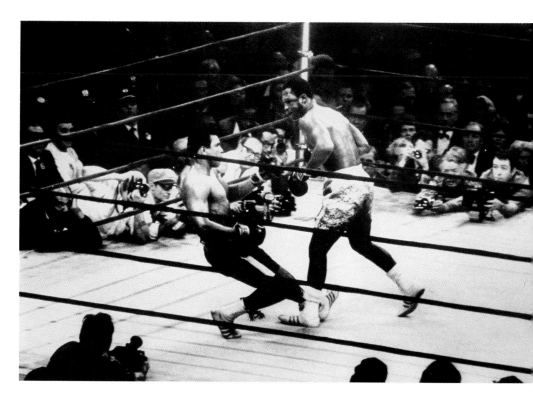

ABOVE / *After Tokyo, Frazier kept running into another American Olympic hero, Muhammad Ali, who won light heavyweight gold as Cassius Clay in Rome in 1960. Here, they're in battle in New York's Madison Square Garden with the world heavyweight championship on the line. Frazier prevailed.* ALLSPORT/HULTON DEUTSCH

ABOVE / *Joe Frazier broke his thumb in this semifinal bout with Russian heavyweight Vadim Yemelyanov, but kept the injury quiet until he had dispatched of Germany's Hans Huber in the gold-medal bout 24 hours later.* ALLSPORT

Dressed to kill (the clock, that is), the sleekly outfitted Italian team of Adler Capelli, Andrea Collinelli, Maruo Trentini and Cristiano Citton only managed a fourth-place showing in the 4,000-meter team pursuit race in Atlanta. ALLSPORT/BARON

Doughnut or diver? Judges watch the three-meter springboard competition in Atlanta. **ALLSPORT/FORSTER**

ABOVE / *French legs.* ALLSPORT/RONDEAU

OPPOSITE / *Owner: Curt Harnett. Canada's premier cyclist won the silver in the 1,000-meter time trial in Los Angeles in 1984, a bronze in the match sprint in Barcelona in 1992, and in 1996 in Atlanta, those 31-year-old legs carried him to another bronze in the match sprint.* ALLSPORT/BRUTY

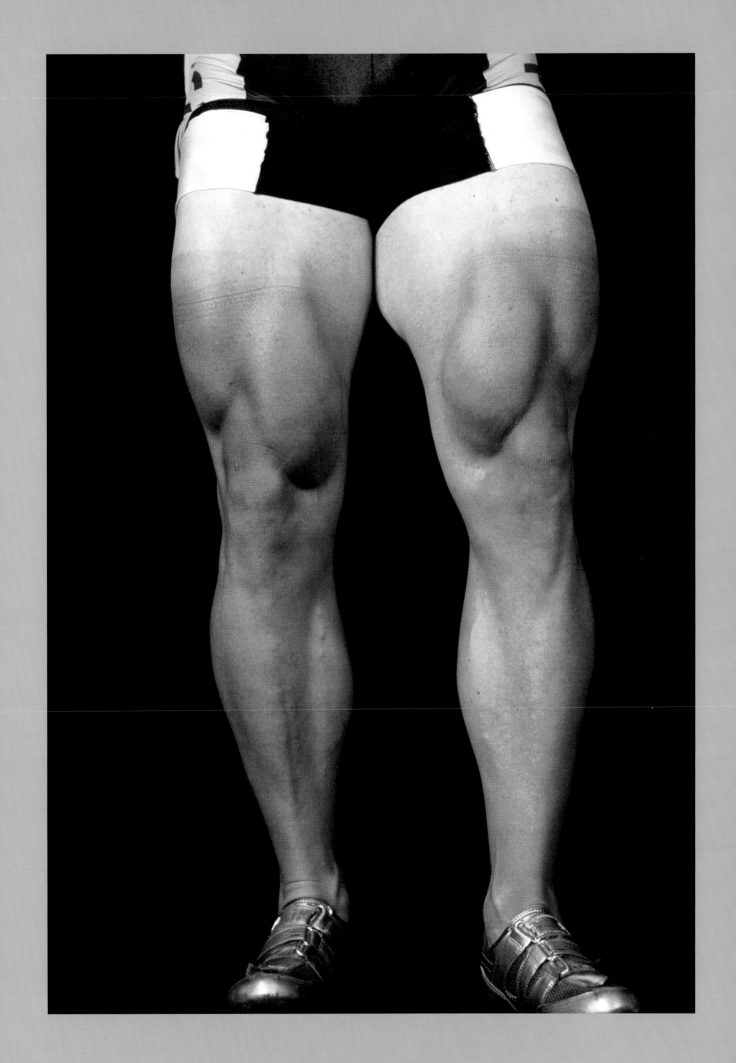

M a r k . S p i t z

THE SPITZING IMAGE

By the time Mark Spitz was old enough to drive a car, he had spent more than three thousand hours in a swimming pool in his native California. By the time he was old enough to vote, he had logged another thousand hours, at least.

Throw in a liberal dose of God-given talent, a swimmer's angular, flexible body, and quality coaching, and the net result of all that pool time was that by the time he was 18 years of age, Spitz was at the very top of his sport. The unquestioned top male swimmer in the world. The holder of numerous world records. The winner of no less than five gold medals at the 1967 Pan American Games.

And on the eve of the 1968 Olympic Games in Mexico City, the surest "sure thing" in the meet.

There wasn't a reputable swimming forecaster in the world who didn't see a Mark Spitz domination in Mexico.

Chief among these forecasters was Spitz himself. With a brashness reserved for the young and bold, he swaggered into Mexico City with a personal prediction that he would win six gold medals in the pool, a haul that would exceed his Pan-Am haul by one.

Not only that, the six gold medals – if accomplished – would also be the largest individual collection in one Games for any Olympian, in any sport, in modern Olympic history.

Thus propped up to such a dizzying height of expectation, Spitz proceeded to fall flat on his face, relatively speaking. When the ripples finally settled after the conclusion of the 1968 swimming competition, the California teenager had just two gold medals to show for his efforts, and even those came partly thanks to his teammates in the 4x100 and 4x200 freestyle relays.

On his own, he was a shadow of his former dominance.

He managed a silver medal in the 100-meter butterfly and a bronze medal in the 100-meter freestyle, but failed to medal at all in the 200-meter butterfly, finishing eighth, nearly five seconds behind U.S. teammate Carl Robie. The butterfly events were especially discouraging. Spitz held world records in both the 100 and 200 coming into the Games, and the loss in the 100 to teammate Douglas Russell, who had never before managed a win against Spitz, meant

Russell would replace Spitz on the U.S. medley relay team (which went on to win the gold medal in world-record time).

Although he returned to California with four medals, the Mexico City Games, by any measure, were a huge disappointment for Mark Spitz.

Approaching the Munich Games four years later, by now an older-and-much-wiser 22, he refused to predict he would win a single gold medal. He won seven.

His was a performance for the ages, not just ranking up there with the Weissmullers and Kahanamokus, but surpassing them all. Not only did Spitz win seven gold medals, one for every time he dove in the water for a final, he also set seven world records. He was untouchable. By anyone. Anytime. The Mexico setback prepared him well.

His opening event in Munich was the 200-meter butterfly – ironically, his last race at Mexico City, where he'd finished eighth. The circumstances were eerily similar. At Munich he was again the world record-holder coming into the Games, having recently lowered his own mark to 2:01.53. Memories of the Mexico debacle reduced Spitz to an openly nervous man as he stood on the

> ## Approaching the Munich Games four years later, by now an older-and-much-wiser 22, he refused to predict he would win a single gold medal. He won seven.

starting block awaiting the starter's gun to sound. Once it did, he was off, leading from start to finish while lowering the world record to 2:00.7. Spitz literally leapt from the water at the finish, both arms thrust high into the air, a salute that tellingly signaled the beginning of a whole new – and much improved – Olympic experience.

Wins in the 100-meter freestyle, 200-meter freestyle, 100-meter butterfly, 4x100-meter freestyle relay, 4x200-meter freestyle relay and 400-meter medley relay soon followed.

Seven races. Seven gold medals. Seven Olympic records. Seven world records. Mark Spitz became the first swimmer to win more than four individual gold medals in a single Olympics, and the first athlete to win seven gold medals, individual and relay team combined, in a single Olympics. Magazines all over the world, sports-oriented and otherwise, suddenly had Mark Spitz on the cover. One of the most famous photographs of the 1972

Games showed the lanky 6-foot, 170-pound Spitz with seven gold medals draped around his neck. He was an instant matinee idol, a worldwide celebrity.

Unfortunately, his amazing performance – and gritty comeback – was not the only stunning news to come out of Munich. On Sept. 5, 1972, a band of armed Palestinian terrorists attacked the athletes representing Israel as they slept in the athletes' village. Two Israelis were killed in the village itself and nine more at the Furstenfeldbruck airfield later in the day.

The impact on the ongoing Games was enormous. Security was tightened and extraordinary precautions were taken to especially protect all Jewish athletes at the Games, Israeli-born and otherwise. In this climate, Mark Spitz, the hero of the Games, was required to leave Munich a full twenty-four hours earlier than scheduled, unable to participate in the Closing Ceremonies where he would have surely been accorded a hero's farewell.

Even with five armed guards at his door, the German officials told him his well-being could not be assured. He had first left his marks on the Games of Munich, and then the terrorists had left theirs.

The contrast was as striking as it was ironic. In the land of the Holocaust, athletic achievement attained in accordance with the highest spirit of the Olympic Games had become contrasted with the lowest form of human behavior. The cowardice of a band of terrorists versus the courage, determination, and skill of a single Jewish American swimmer. For better and for worse, neither would soon be forgotten. ▾

ABOVE / *After eating his words in Mexico, a much wiser and older Mark Spitz came to Munich with no gold-medal predictions. He simply showed the world his worth, winning all seven of his races and setting seven world records.* ALLSPORT

RIGHT / Twenty-six-year-old Michelle Smith of Ireland, who wasn't even ranked in the top 20 in the world coming into the 1996 Games, became Atlanta's most decorated individual swimmer. She won three gold medals – in the 400-meter individual medley, the 400-meter freestyle, and the 200-meter freestyle – and a bronze in the 200-meter butterfly, where goggle problems slowed her down. No woman had so dominated the Games since Kristin Otto of East Germany won four individual gold medals in 1988.

Jim . Craig

REALITY ON ICE

The first thing Jim Craig did when his work was done, when the goal crease no longer needed protection, when the defeat of the imperious Soviet Union had been followed by a gold-medal defeat of Finland, was skate around the Olympic Field House rink, looking for his Dad.

Years later, that's still the moment that stands out in many people's minds who first watched, incredulously, either live or on teleivision, the Miracle On Ice 4-3 win over the Soviets, and then, two days later, stood in more awe as the United States hockey team beat back the Finns, four goals to two ...

...A kid looking for his dad.

Not that Jim Craig – at 22, his was the average age of the 20 players who made up the 1980 United States Olympic Hockey Team – exactly qualified as a kid. But in this arena, Craig, and his teammates, were definitely kids. Kids against men. Not only did their European opponents average nearly half a decade older, but when it came to hockey tradition and domination, the difference was very much grownup and child.

Especially when it came to the team from the Soviet Union.

A collection of the very best players from the Central Red Army and Russia's top "amateur" teams, the Moscow Dynamo and the Moscow Wings, the USSR national team had come to Lake Placid tagged as the "best hockey team in the world," a moniker based more on fact than hype given the USSR's domination of a team of National Hockey League All-Stars the winter previous. In that competition – a hockey cultural

> Kids against men. Not only did their Soviet opponents average half a decade older, but when it came to hockey tradition and domination, the difference was very much grownup and child.

exchange called the Challenge Cup played in New York's Madison Square Garden – the NHL got roundly thrashed.

To re-emphasize their superiority, the Soviets had returned to Madison Square Garden a year later, three days before the beginning of the Olympic Games, to face the U.S. team in exhibition. Final score: USSR 10, USA 3.

At least the Americans, unlike those

NHL All-Stars, could take solace in their youth and relative inexperience. While it's true that the team, under the no-nonsense thumb of head coach Herb Brooks, climaxed a winter-long 63-game get-ready-for-the-Games minor league and college campus barnstorming tour with that game against the Soviets, it's also true that no U.S. player had much experience in the upper echelons of the sport.

The U.S. team, consisting chiefly of the country's best college players, reflected the convoluted rules of the times: Only "amateurs" could play in the Olympics (a requirement since rescinded). No professionals – anyone paid to play – allowed.

Of course, the rules of amatuerism also applied to the Soviets, but since hockey in the now defunct USSR was controlled by the state, the state made sure none of its players, although that was their job, made any actual money.

It was this structure that created the USSR's domination of Olympic hockey. Ever since Helsinki, where the first post-Czar Russians competed in 1952, the Soviets had ruled the rinks. In the six Olympic Games leading to Lake Placid, the USSR owned five gold medals and one bronze medal – in 1960 when the United States also managed to buck the odds. Overall, the USSR's Olympic record stood at 33-3-2, with a 255-76 goal-scoring advantage.

Such was the daunting history that greeted the U.S. Olympians. Theirs was a fool's errand. An impossible dream.

Fortunately – for them – they were young enough they didn't know that

what they were trying to do couldn't be done.

Also fortunately, they had a hot goalkeeper.

As any hockey player worth his mouthpiece will attest, there is nothing more valuable than a goalie who is in the zone.

Craig, the U.S. goalie, was in the zone. Not necessarily when the games would start. In the early going, he was just ordinary.

But once the U.S. got behind, he was virtually impenetrable. With the exception of a 7-2 romp over Romania, in every game played in the Olympic tournament – eight in all – the U.S. would come from behind. When the going got serious, the U.S. would score ... and Jim Craig would get stingy.

In nearly every regard, Craig epitomized the American team. After an outstanding college career at Boston University, where he played on an NCAA championship team in 1978, he held off turning pro. It wasn't an easy decision. The NHL's Atlanta Flames had chosen him in the

fourth round of the pro draft following his sophomore season. With his father out of work at the time, and just months following his mother's death from cancer, Jim, the sixth of eight brothers and sisters, was tempted to sign.

Many on that '80 squad carried similar dossiers. In essence, they each gave a winter of their hockey careers to their country.

It was a like-minded group that skated into the semifinal game against the Soviets, where, right on cue, the U.S. fell behind, first 1-0, then 2-1, then 3-2.

But then came the decisive third period, and with more than 10,000 people, 1,500 beyond capacity, packed into the Field House – each one, it seemed, carrying an American Flag – that third period belonged to Jim Craig & Company. First, Mark Johnson tied the score, 3-3; then, 81 seconds later, Mike Eruzione sent the U.S. into the lead with a 30-foot slapshot.

In the 10 minutes that followed, with the crowd on its feet, Jim Craig took over.

As the best hockey team in the world flailed away, often breaking ranks in an attempt to storm from behind, he denied anything and everything. In all, he would stop 36 Soviet shots in the game, nine in the final period.

The Americans had their miracle.

And 48 hours after that, after holding off the Finns, they had their gold medal.

That's when Jim Craig broke ranks, eschewing the wild celebration that began in a tiny rink in Lake Placid and instantaneously spread to an entire nation. That's when he left his post and went searching, and gave the Olympics a snapshot to be remembered ...

... Before he shared what he was feeling with the world, the kid who shut down first the Russians, and then the Finns, wanted to share it with his Dad. ▼

ABOVE / *The seasoned Soviets came to Lake Placid to pocket another gold in ice hockey, but were humbled by a bunch of American kids, 4-3, and left with a bronze-colored memento.* ALLSPORT/S. POWELL

In Atlanta, the men's final game pitted Sweden versus Croatia, with the Croats edging the Swedes by a single point, 27-26. Yugoslavia had been a traditional powerhouse in team handball, winning the gold in 1972 and 1984 and the bronze in 1988. With the redefinition of borders, Croatia seemed to have inherited the talent. Sweden got another taste of "always the bridesmaid, never the bride" having won the silver in Barcelona as well. ALLSPORT/HEWITT

In the 57 kilogram (125.5 pound) division of Greco-Roman wrestling, American Dennis Hall, a 1995 world champion, met the person he defeated for that world title, Yurij Melnichenko of Kazakhstan, for the Olympic gold medal in Atlanta. This time, however, Melnichenko, the 1994 world champ, prevailed, winning 4-1. ALLSPORT/LEAH

A new definition of the uphill battle: Nordic skiers in the men's 15-kilometer pursuit race get an adrenalin boost from the cheering crowd at Lillehammer. Norwegian Bjorn Daehlie leads the charge from start to finish, winning almost a half minute in front of silver medalist Vladimir Smirnov of Kazakhstan.

ALLSPORT/COLE

P h i l . M a h r e

THIRD TIME'S A CHARM

For more than half a decade as the 1970s turned into the 1980s, Phil Mahre and his identical twin brother, Steve, did something rare for American ski racers – they struck fear into the rest of the world. If Phil, a three-time overall World Cup champion from 1981 through 1983, wasn't climbing to the top of the winner's podium, Steve, a nine-time individual champion, was. The look-alikes from Washington State – where they were raised in a house some 30 yards from the ski lift at the White Pass Ski Area – were often the scourge of the tour, even if they were Americans.

There was certainly no precedent for such dominance by American male ski racers on the world-class circuit. In nearly 50 years of alpine racing, only a handful of American men had ever made their presence felt, and it was typically brief.

But for all their brash comeuppance, the Mahres had an Achilles' heel: The Olympic Games. Whenever the World Cup made its quadrennial Olympic stop, Phil and Steve tended to blend into the crowd. They first went to the Winter Games as on-the-rise 18-year-olds in

Innsbruck in 1976, where they failed to medal, or even come close. Their next Olympic stop was Lake Placid, New York, in 1980, where, despite being home-nation favorites, they were nearly shutout again. A silver-medal performance by Phil in the final event, the slalom, was reason for some celebration, but the fact he yielded the lead after the first run to Sweden's Ingemar Stenmark, who had already won the giant slalom three days earlier, was not. With the Games on American snow for the first time in 20 years, expectations going in were high that an American male – read: the Mahres – would finally, for the first time in history, claim a gold medal in downhill skiing, thereby ending America's Olympic drought.

As it was, Phil's slalom silver medal would only equal the silver medal won at Innsbruck in 1964 by slalomist Billy Kidd.

By the time the next Olympic Winter Games rolled around in 1984 in Sarajevo, the plot, and pressure, had only thickened. By now, the Mahre brothers in general, and Phil in particular, were established among the best ski racers of all-time. Without argument, Phil had taken over from Stenmark as the "world's best skier." When he captured his third straight overall World Cup championship

(signifying overall supremacy in the three disciplines of slalom, giant slalom and downhill) following the 1983 season he joined just two other racers, Italy's Gustavo Thoeni and Stenmark, who had also managed to win three straight Cup crowns. Despite a lack of Olympic gold, Phil Mahre was very much a racer for the ages.

Occasionally, Phil recoiled at the prevail-ing public perception in the United States that his career was somehow unfulfilled because of his lack of Olympic success. The Winter Games, he would point out, were merely one stop on the World Cup circuit – and not even a year-ly stop at that. To base a racer's reputation on how he, or she, fared at one competition every four years was hardly fair, Mahre reasoned. He was right, of course. He was also hopelessly outnumbered. No matter how often, or efficiently, he pointed out the inconsistencies in the "weighting" of the Olympic ski races, in his home country, especially, the Winter Games would nonetheless get the lion's share of the attention.

Thus, it was hardly surprising that when the Sarajevo Games opened with the giant slalom and Phil finished in eighth place, and Steve in 17th, those results

A storm raged and blanketed the twisting, technical course with heavy snow. Of 101 entrants in the race that day, 54 wouldn't even finish.

turned ... in the Mahres' favor.

This was the kind of a race the brothers could get their teeth into.

Olympics or not.

After the first run, with racer after racer abandoning the gates, Steve stood in first place and Phil in third, separated only by a young Swedish racer, Jonas Nilsson.

Phil was the first of the twins to race his second run, going out just ahead of Nilsson and Steve. He quickly skied into the No. 1 position, at least a bronze medal already in the bag. By the time Nilsson crossed the finish line a moment later, after an erratic descent, Phil's bronze had turned to silver. It could turn to gold, depending on how his brother, now entering the gate atop the course, fared. Phil grabbed a walkie-talkie and hurriedly shouted advice on how to ski the course to Steve. He could think of no one he'd rather finished behind.

Holding nothing back, Steve rocketed down the course. His two-run total time wound up beating everybody ... except his brother. The final results showed Philip Mahre with a clocking of 1:39.41 and Steven Mahre just behind at 1:39.62. Didier Bouvet, a Frenchman, finished well back at 1:40.20 to get the bronze, with Nilsson another five-hundredths of a second back.

At last, America had its first-ever Olympic gold medal in men's slalom racing, and its first-ever one-two finish in any alpine event. And the Mahre brothers, they had finally beaten their Olympic jinx, even if they never gave it much credence in the first place. ▼

were received with more attention, and derision, than any of the brothers' dozens of World Cup wins that had come before.

The Mahres and their Olympic jinx, it appeared, were obviously alive and well. And to make the American mood even less hopeful, Phil Mahre, when interviewed by the media after the less-than-anticipated giant slalom results, insisted on re-emphasizing his comments concerning the relative unimportance of

winning at the Olympics.

Five days after the giant slalom, the Sarajevo Games were poised to close with the running of the slalom down the steep pitch of Mt. Bjelasnica. A storm raged and blanketed the twisting, technical course with heavy snow – setting up conditions hardly conducive to pleasant racing. Of 101 entrants in the race that day, 54 wouldn't even finish.

As it turned out, the tide had finally

LEFT / With the end in sight and leading the competition coming into the final event of the modern pentathlon, the 4,000-meter cross country run, Russian Eduard Zenovka breaks away from Aleksandr Parygin, only to collapse moments later, giving the man from Kazakhstan a date with the gold. The exhausted Zenovka crept across the finish line to claim the silver before he was carried away. In Atlanta, in an effort to preserve and liven up the five-event sport originally introduced by Pierre de Coubertin, the schedule was streamlined into an exhausting one-day event. ALLSPORT/FORSTER

RIGHT / Equestrian — where rider and horse blur as one to compete for the gold.
ALLSPORT/HEWITT

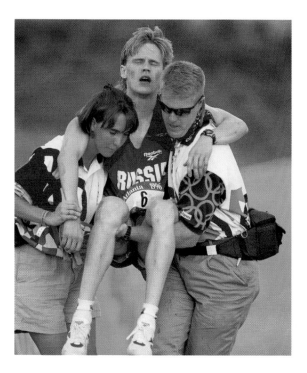

Valerie . Brisco

BACK ON TRACK

The year 1960 was a banner one for women's track and field in the United States. First, sprinter Wilma Rudolph won three gold medals at the Rome Olympics. Second, Valerie Brisco was born.

Rudolph's success was unprecedented – no American woman had ever won three gold medals in a single Olympics – and she became an international star. This remarkably talented and graceful African-American's life story was soon on film and in print. Her book became a staple of many a schoolhouse library in the United States. A few years later, schoolgirl Valerie Brisco, growing up in the tough, hard streets of the Watts section of Los Angeles, read that book. She already had an idea she was a fast runner, faster in fact than all the boys in her class. God had given Valerie Brisco speed. The Wilma Rudolph story gave her inspiration.

When Valerie was only nine years old, her older brother, Robert, a track star at Locke High School, was killed by a stray bullet while he was jogging on the high school track. Valerie was especially close to Robert, who always encouraged his little sister to participate in sports. The tragic incident further fueled Valerie's desire to be a champion sprinter. They renamed the Locke High School track in honor of Robert Brisco, and it was on that surface where Valerie Brisco became a phenomenal high school track star. The best in the entire nation. As a high school sophomore in 1975, she ran the 400 meters in a remarkable 54.19 seconds – barely three seconds beyond the existing world record. By the time she graduated, she lowered her own record time to 52.08 seconds, easily the fastest schoolgirl in the U.S.

Accepting the fact that her biggest shortcoming was an aversion to hard training, and realizing she couldn't continue to progress on God-given talent alone, Valerie accepted a college track scholarship at California State Northridge University, not far from her home, where she knew her tendency to "chill out" would be more than countered by the work ethic of Northridge's head coach, a no-nonsense man with a drill sergeant air named Bob Kersee.

The formula worked. At Northridge, Kersee had Valerie lifting weights up to three hours a day and concluding each workout with 250 pushups and a 1,000 sit-ups. The hard work paid off. By the time she was 19, she won a national championship at 200 meters and a gold medal at the same distance at the 1979 Pan American Games. Another gold medal – of the Olympic variety – might have soon followed, but the American boycott of the 1980 Moscow Games effectively eliminated that possibility.

A year later, it appeared that any designs Valerie might have on an Olympic medal were now a thing of the past. After marrying professional football player Alvin Hooks in 1980, she gave birth to their son, Alvin Jr., in 1981. Forty pounds added by the pregnancy did not come off. The added weight, along with the demands and distractions of motherhood, combined to put an end to Valerie's running career.

But when her son was two years old, she decided she still had something to prove on the track. She decided she still wanted to become the next Wilma Rudolph. And if Wilma Rudolph could come back from giving birth to become a champion

> When her son was two years old, she decided she still had something to prove on the track. With her old coach personally overseeing her training regimen, she lost those 40 post-pregnancy pounds in only two months.

– indeed, Wilma, who gave birth to her first child at 17, two years before the Rome Games, did just that – well, she could, too.

The person who hated to train again turned to her solution – Bob Kersee. With her old coach personally overseeing her training regimen, she lost those 40 post-pregnancy pounds in only two months. Then, with her weight down, she took to her old training routine with her sights set on the Olympic Games scheduled for Los Angeles – her hometown – in a little less than a year.

Unlike most other sprinters, Valerie chose to compete in races right up to the Olympic Trials. She needed to run. She needed to catch up. Her strategy paid off. She set a U.S. record in the 200 meters a week before the Trials, where she was able to easily qualify for the U.S. Olympic Team. When the Olympics descended on Los Angeles less than a month later, she was peaked and ready to fly.

The track events in L.A. were held at the venerable Memorial Coliseum, site of the 1932 Games, and it was there, just three miles from the Robert Brisco Memorial Track at Locke High School, that Valerie Brisco, running with her hair in standard cornrows, indeed became the next Wilma Rudolph.

First she won the 400 meters in the Olympic- and American-record time of 48.83 seconds, nosing out her teammate, U.S. record-holder Chandra Cheeseborough, in the process.

Three days later, she won the 200 meters in 21.81 seconds, again setting Olympic and American records as she became the first Olympian to win at 200 and 400 meters in the same Games. (Twelve years later, in the 1996 Centennial Games in Atlanta, Michael Johnson of the United States would become the first man to achieve the elusive 200-400 "double," a feat that would be attended by consider-

ably more fanfare).

Finally, she and her U.S. teammates – including Cheeseborough, Sherrie Howard and Lillie Leatherwood – conspired to win the 1,600-meter relay. Valerie ran the third leg as the American team clocked 3:18.29 to set yet another Olympic record and blaze to a finish nearly two full seconds in front of the silver-medalist team from Canada.

Thus it was that Valerie Brisco became the first American woman – and mother – to win three gold medals in a single Olympics since her childhood idol, Wilma Rudolph, did it way back in 1960, the year Valerie was born. In the final result, it was clearly a case of one great athlete emulating another – and doing it by the book. ▼

ABOVE / *Valerie Brisco was the first woman to win the 200-400 meter double in Olympic history in 1984. Back four years later in Seoul, Brisco helped the 4x400-meter relay team to a silver medal.*
ALLSPORT/M. POWELL

In Calgary in 1988, Vreni Schneider won the slalom and the giant slalom. In Albertville in 1992, there were no medals for the Swiss skier. But in Lillehammer, Schneider was a serious threat and added another gold in the slalom, a silver in the women's combined and a bronze in the giant slalom to her Olympic collection.
ALLSPORT/BILOW

L a u n i . M e i l i

PRESSURE
SHOOTING

L auni Meili, the best woman with a rifle anyone in Cheney, Wash., had ever seen, had a problem on her hands. Going into the 20-minute, 10-shot final round of the women's small bore three-position rifle final at the Olympic Games in Barcelona, Spain, the pride of Cheney was in first place, a full two points ahead of the field.

Normally, first place with a healthy lead is exactly where you want to be.

But for Meili, it had never worked out that way before.

The three-position rifle competition marked the end of a long two-Olympic, four-event road for Meili (pronounced "My-Lee"), and despite her excellent standing going into what she knew would be her "final final" (her retirement plans were firm; after Barcelona she would go home, buy a house, and make pots), she had every reason to suspect a nightmare ending awaited. Make that another nightmare ending. By now, she was used to them. Boy, was she! This leading business had thus far been very, very bad for her.

As hard as she – and anyone familiar with her story – tried not to, as she waited for the final, it was impossible not to reflect on what had happened before:

In the 1988 Games in Seoul, in her first Olympic appearance after five national American championships, she began in the air rifle competition. She started off like a 25-year-old world-beater, scoring 396 points in the opening round qualifying for the eight-woman finals in first place with a new Olympic record to her credit (the old record was 393). In the finals, however, Meili faded badly. Her hand shook, her eye left her, her bullets went everywhere. She wound up finishing sixth, out of eight, a lengthy 2.5 points away from a bronze medal ... and a complete basket case, besides.

Three days after Seoul's air rifle competition, it was a rejuvenated and doubly determined Meili who showed up for the small bore three-position rifle competition. In the opening round, she moved through the three positions – prone, kneeling and standing – like she owned the range, scoring 582 points, once again qualifying for the eight-woman finals in first place with a new Olympic record to her credit (the old record was 581). In the finals, however, Meili faded badly. Her hand shook, her eye left her, her bullets went everywhere. She wound up finishing seventh, out of eight, a lengthy five points out of a bronze medal. Déjà vu, all over again.

> Normally, first place with a healthy lead is exactly where you want to be. But for Meili, it had never worked out that way before.

Of all the long plane rides back home from Seoul, Launi Meili's may have been the longest.

But she refused to quit. She kept shooting and got her aim back (an air rifle win in the 1988 World Cup helped) and, convinced that she'd "obsessed with shooting too much," determined that, although she still wanted to try for another Olympics, she'd "round out" her life. She got more hobbies. She became an aerobics instructor. She went back to her hometown college, Eastern Washington University, and got her degree in nutrition and exercise science. She met Leo Lachambre in Colorado Springs in 1989 and they were married. He hung up her bull's-eyes from competitions around the house to help her confidence.

To improve her nerves, she worked at relaxation and visualizing techniques. "You have to learn to work with the pressure," she told a reporter at the USOC training center in Colorado Springs in 1990, "so when you're finally there again you feel like you've handled it a thousand times."

It was as a determined 29-year-old veteran that she returned to the Olympics in Barcelona in 1992.

Her first event, the air rifle, was sched-

uled for the first day of competition, Sunday, July 26th. That was good. She wouldn't have to sit around the Olympic Village, waiting, allowing the pressure to build.

In the air rifle, she decided to pace herself in the opening round. But she opened too slowly and when the shooting was over she found herself in a tie for 11th place, her score of 391 leaving her one point away from qualifying for the medal round as one of the top eight shooters.

The good news was that, for once, she wouldn't enter the frenetic 20-minute, 10-shot final round as the marskwoman to beat.

The bad news was that she wouldn't be entering it at all.

When Launi Meili finally arrived at the three-position rifle competition four days later, on Thursday, July 30th, she was hauling a lot of baggage with her.

And when she resumed her Seoul ways and charged to the front with her field-leading 587 in the opening round – yet another Olympic record – she dragged all that baggage into her final round as well. What else was she going to do with it?

Even her biggest fans and supporters – a group led by her father, Hal Meili, who first put a rifle in his daughter's hands at his gun club in Spokane when she was a seventh grader dreaming of making the Olympics as an ice skater – had a hard time looking. The wait between the prelims and the finals was excruciating. For all of them. Team Meili had been here before. It wasn't crunch time as much as it was cringe time.

But then came the best 20 minutes of shooting Launi Meili had ever done. Her hand was steady, her eyes dead on.

She opened with a bull's-eye and never looked back. She wasn't perfect, but she

was close. Her final round score of 97.3 and her total score of 684.3 both established Olympic records – the fourth and fifth times she could say that as an Olympian – and her final position qualified her for a gold medal – the first time as an Olympian she could say that.

As she mounted the winner's peristyle and they raised the United States flag and played the national anthem, Launi Meili bit her lip but it didn't come close to stopping the tears.

"This," she said afterward, still crying openly, "is the dream of a lifetime come true." No one doubted that she'd earned the tears. ▼

ABOVE / After a heartbreaking loss in Seoul, Launi Meili returned to Barcelona with a new air of determination that clinched the gold in the three-position rifle competition.
ALLSPORT/MORTIMORE

LEFT /A picture of concentration: Susi Susanti of Indonesia, Barcelona's badminton queen ALLSPORT/BOTTERILL; America's Andre Agassi (below left), king of the courts in Atlanta ALLSPORT/LEAH; and Ghana's Kwame Ayew, making headway in the soccer world with an Olympic bronze in Barcelona. ALLSPORT/CANNON

OPPOSITE / Behind the arm strength of its pitchers and the caliber of Osvaldo Fernando, Cuba quickly established itself as baseball's best by going undefeated in the inaugural Olympic baseball tournament in Barcelona. ALLSPORT/M. POWELL

D a n . J a n s e n

GOING
WITH THE
FLOW

At the 1988 Olympic Winter Games in Calgary, speed skater Dan Jansen was expected to win. Just three weeks earlier, he had beaten the best skaters in the world at the World Sprint Championships, winning decisively at both 500 and 1,000 meters. At 22, and a skater since he was four, he was the acknowledged fastest in the world. Four years earlier at the Sarajevo Games, he had placed fourth in the 500, just missing out on the bronze medal, which even then had been something of a disappointment. In the ensuing four years, Dan Jansen of West Allis, Wis., had refined his form and dominated his sport. In Calgary, he was poised to win.

Then, the morning the competition was to begin, his sister died.

It was Valentine's Day, 1988, at 8:50 a.m. when Jane Jansen passed away. She had fought a fierce battle with leukemia and had spent her last few weeks in a hospital bed in Wisconsin while she watched her brother prepare for the Olympics. She and Dan had always been close and

both raced as children. Dan stayed with the sport and Jane married a fireman and became a mother of three. Now she was dead at 27, and the 500-meter sprint was scheduled for that same afternoon.

Dan and Jane had spoken on the telephone just three hours before she died. She told Dan to race, that was her desire. And so he did. He would race this race like he had never raced before and he would win it for his sister. He took his practice laps, and at 5:10 p.m., just eight hours after Jane's death, he toed the starting line with a pale face and a heavy heart. His father, Harry, later said, "he was thinking about Jane. I knew he'd either fall, or he'd skate the race of his life."

He fell. Thirteen seconds and 100 meters into the race, Jansen's left skate crumpled beneath him and he crashed sideways into the foam barrier surrounding the rink. Dan Jansen, the world champion, emerged from Calgary with no gold medals – no medals at all. And an entire nation felt his pain.

After Calgary, Dan Jansen did what he had always done. He continued to skate. By the time he arrived in Albertville four

years later, for the 1992 Winter Games, he had even better credentials than in Calgary. Just three weeks earlier he had lowered the world record in the 500 to 36.41. And after what had happened in Calgary, the public interest was tremendous. Everyone was pulling for Dan Jansen. Suddenly, speed skating had become one of the most-watched competitions of the Games.

In the 500, Jansen started out fast, but he hesitated slightly at the far turn and never caught back up, finishing in 37.46, good enough for only fourth place. Three days later, in the 1,000, he was even worse, fading to 26th. After three Olympic Games and six Olympic races, the best speed skater alive had no medals. No one could explain it, certainly not Jansen himself. "Maybe," he said, "it is not meant to be."

Still, in 1994 in Lillehammer, he tried again. By that time he had more than 50 World Cup medals and a succession of world records. Just weeks earlier, he had become the first skater in history to crack the 35-second barrier in the 500. But age was taking its toll in this young

> Dan Jansen did himself a favor. He didn't care anymore. Not that he wouldn't do his best, not that he wouldn't try to win, not that he didn't *want* to win, but it hit him, and hit him good, that he didn't *have* to win.

man's sport, and these would undoubtedly be Jansen's last Olympic Games. It had to be now. The 500 meters had always been his best event and as he assumed his position for the 500 in Norway a worldwide audience looked on.

On the third turn of the race, a turn where Jansen had never slipped before, he slipped, and it cost him the race. He finished eighth. And the whole world groaned. Dan himself felt so badly after the event that he canceled a planned formal interview. He just couldn't face the public.

Then reality really set in. Through seven races in the Olympics he had failed to win a single medal. He had failed to win for his country, he had failed to win for the people back home in Wisconsin ("Sorry, Milwaukee" he apologized to a reporter after the Calgary Games), and he had failed to win for his sister. And then, with only the 1,000-meter race left, and with all of his earlier concerns about

letting everyone down, Dan Jansen did himself a favor. He didn't care anymore. Not that he wouldn't do his best, not that he wouldn't try to win, not that he didn't *want* to win, but it hit him, and hit him good, that he didn't *have* to win. In fact, he didn't expect to anymore. He wasn't even the favorite in the 1,000, that distinction going to Igor Zhelevosky of Belarus, who held the world record. "The way I got relaxed," he said, "was not to care."

Then the 1,000-meter race began. This time Dan didn't go out too fast. He wanted to, some part of him still wanted to rush the start, to push too hard, but he held back and he was skating good, he could feel it, and so could his wife, Robin, up in the stands. And so could the world, but not too much, because this was Dan Jansen out there, and disaster could strike at any second. And on the second to the last turn he did slip, his left hand grazing the ice, but this time he didn't fall, he kept his balance, kept his

rhythm, and the man who didn't care so much anymore got stronger and this time wound up skating the race of his life. He cruised down the final straightaway in a blur, crossing the finish line just ahead of Zhelevosky. Dan Jansen had just won the gold medal, set a world record, and finally excised the demons that day in Norway. And he did it for himself.

"This time," his coach said, "the man upstairs took care of him."

Jansen moved to the stands where he kissed his wife and took their nine-month-old daughter into his arms. As the crowd rose in a thundering tribute, together they skated a victory lap, Jansen and the little girl, whose name was Jane. ▼

ABOVE / *After 16 years and repeated heart-wrenching disappointments in the Olympic Winter Games, Dan Jansen, along with the world who watched, celebrated his 1,000-meter speed skating victory in Lillehammer.* ALLSPORT/COLE

Mozambique's Maria Mutola (3569) and Ana Quirot of Cuba (left) were heavily favored to take the top two spots in the 800-meter race in Atlanta, but while the pack waited for the two to start the homestretch kick, Russia's Svetlana Masterkova (3700) beat them to it. She sprinted to the finish first, leaving Quirot in second and Mutola in third.

ALLSPORT/MORTIMORE

Teresa Edwards

BURDEN OF PROOF

With an Olympic medal collection including two gold medals; with a pair of consensus All-America awards at the University of Georgia to her credit; with a nine-year professional career in Italy, Spain, France and Japan behind her; with the unofficial title of "The First Lady of Basketball," it would seem safe to assume that when Teresa Edwards led the United States women's basketball team into Atlanta for the Centennial Olympic Games she came simply to take a bow.

That assumption would be wrong.

Despite everywhere she'd been and everything she'd done, when the 5-foot-11 Edwards set down her bags in Atlanta, not far from her girlhood home of Cairo, Georgia, she unpacked plenty left to prove. Maybe she was the well-decorated veteran. Maybe she had been a member of the first U.S. women's team ever to win an Olympic gold medal – in Los Angeles in '84. And maybe she had followed that up with another gold medal in Seoul in '88. But for one thing, the deco-

rations and the medals were not nearly modern enough. Teresa had also been on the U.S. team that slipped to a bronze-medal finish in the 1992 Games in Barcelona; and she followed that up as a

ABOVE / *Teresa Edwards helped lead the U.S. women's basketball team to a gold-medal victory over Brazil, the same team that had beaten the Americans at the world championships in 1994.* ALLSPORT/PENSINGER

member of the U.S. team that lost to Brazil in the 1994 World Championship finals. That is what she'd done lately.

To make matters more difficult, during the same period of time that the U.S. women were losing their reputation as best-in-the-world, the U.S. men were getting theirs back. It was in Barcelona that the U.S. men's "Dream Team" avenged a bronze-medal U.S. finish four years before in Seoul, and it was at the '94 Worlds that another Dream Team version waltzed to the gold medal.

Nobody had to spell it out for the U.S. women as the countdown for Atlanta began: If they wanted their reputation back, they knew where, and how, they could earn it.

As the lone link between the good ol' gold-medal days and the present, the challenge for Edwards was also personal. Her country's return to glory would signal her individual return to glory as well.

It was, of course, aggravating to have to pay the price ... again. Under fairer circumstances, Edwards would have long ago been acknowledged as the top point guard in U.S. women's history, regardless of any Olympic Games outcome. At the age of 32, you name it – stats, titles, longevity – she had done it. The problem was *where* she had done it. After a sterling college career at Georgia that ended in 1986 and included school records in steals and assists, two NCAA Final Four appearances and the retiring of her number (5), she had moved on to play professionally in Italy, Japan, Spain and France. Year-in, year-out, she would lead her teams in scoring and assists in exchange for strange food and a nice paycheck. But for very little notoriety, particularly in her homeland – where no professional job opportunities existed.

She was able to make a nice living. After a couple of seasons she bought her mother – who raised Teresa and her four younger brothers by herself – a new house in Cairo.

But if the money was good, it wasn't everything. She proved that when she turned down a reported $100,000 offer to play in France during the Olympic year and instead accepted a $50,000 offer to play a full barnstorming season for the U.S. national team. For half the pay, she agreed to work twice as hard, embarking on a 52-game, four-continent nearly year-long warm-up tour.

Led by their well-known world traveler, the U.S. team got ready for the Atlanta

Nobody had to spell it out for the U.S. women as the countdown for Atlanta began: If they wanted their reputation back, they knew where, and how, they could earn it.

Games by winning all 52 of those barnstorming games. Some of the tune-up wins came in Siberia, others in China, others in Australia. By the time the women arrived in Atlanta, they had traveled more than 100,000 miles just to get there.

In tribute to Edwards' fourth appearance in the Olympics, as well as her Georgia roots, she was given the honor of reciting, on behalf of all the world's athletes, the Athletes' Oath at the Opening Ceremonies. In front of a record television audience in excess of an estimated one billion, she performed flawlessly, not missing a word.

It was a harbinger of what was to come.

As the U.S. women proceeded to play to capacity crowds at first the Morehouse College Gymnasium and then the 32,000-seat Georgia Dome – where the largest crowds to ever watch women's basketball assembled daily – Edwards was at her point-guard best. She led the American team with a tournament-leading eight assists per game while averaging 6.9 points on 60 percent shooting. She might have scored more, but after carrying much of the offensive load in Seoul and Barcelona – where she averaged 16.6 and 12.6 points, respectively – she found it wasn't necessary in Atlanta. Neither was she required to play as many minutes. And for good reason.

Nobody came close to the Americans.

The U.S. women won eight straight Olympic contests by an average of 28 points. Their smallest margin of victory was a 15-point win over Japan and their 60-point win over Zaire was the largest. Edwards' typical role was to start the games, set the pace, establish a dominating lead, and then turn over the game to her understudies at the point.

Not that she wasn't above an individual outburst or two. Against Australia she went on a 15-assist, 20-point binge that included seven-of-eight shooting.

In the gold-medal game against essentially the same Brazilian team that had come back from a 20-point deficit to beat the Americans in the 1994 world championships, Edwards had 10 assists, nine points, four rebounds and two steals – more than enough to pace a 111-87 triumph.

"I can't top what's happened today," said a jubilant – and relieved – Edwards in the euphoric afterglow of that gold-medal win over Brazil. "We had a lot on our shoulders. We just had to cap it all off with this gold medal. We really had to."

It was what she – and they – had come to Atlanta to prove. ▼

Eyes on the road: At the 50-kilometer points race in Seoul, the peloton successfully maneuvers a curve.
ALLSPORT/VANDYSTADT

ALLSPORT/FORSTER

With the Olympic stage as their backdrop, athletes in Atlanta gracefully sign the distinctive signatures of their sports. ALLSPORT/HEWITT

Dan . O ' Brien

SETTLING THE SCORE

In New Orleans at the 1992 United States Olympic Trials, the question was not whether Dan O'Brien would make the team, but whether he would set a world record in the process.

It was well known that O'Brien had paid his dues ... and then some. Here was a self-made success story if track and field had ever seen one. O'Brien had personally overseen his reconstruction from a down-and-out loser to perhaps the brightest prospect on the entire American team. Slightly less than ten years earlier, he and the University of Idaho, where he'd held a track scholarship, had parted company, and not on the best of terms. From 1984 through 1987, he didn't attend school at all, or compete on the track either. He'd more or less bottomed out in Christmas of 1987, unemployed, broke, and with a drinking problem.

Resigned that he could go no lower, it was then that O'Brien went on his own crusade to get himself back together. With the help of his former track coach at Idaho, Mike Keller – who was willing, but hardly optimistic – he got back into school at nearby Spokane Community College. A career, however fledgling, was reborn. And quickly. By the time of the 1988 U.S. Olympic Trials less than a year later, O'Brien's decathlon marks were impressive enough that he was at least invited to the meet.

After college, Keller took over as O'Brien's personal coach and soon enough O'Brien was challenging the best decathlete in the country, a Californian named Dave Johnson. In their first head-to-head competition at the national championships in 1990, Johnson prevailed, but barely, winning with a final score of 8,600 points, just 117 points in front of O'Brien's 8,483.

The prospect that the world's two best decathletes were emerging from one nation caught the attention of Reebok, the shoe company giant. Anticipating a rivalry that would only get more intense, Reebok developed one of the most expensive sports advertising campaigns in history, with a budget of $25 million, focusing solely on these two decathletes. The campaign featured a series of videos that asked "Dave or Dan, who is the world's greatest athlete?" and ended with the intriguing promise: "To be settled in Barcelona," site of the upcoming 1992 Olympic Games. The ads opened with huge fanfare during the 1992 Super Bowl. Over the coming months, an estimated 1.2 billion people around the world would watch them.

Many mortals might have called it a career then and there. But anyone who saw what O'Brien did immediately following the pole vault debacle got a preview of his character.

It was at this juncture that the U.S. Olympic Trials – considered a mere qualification formality for both Dave and Dan – arrived. After the first of two days of decathlon competition, O'Brien took the lead, on pace for a near world-record performance.

But on the second day came the pole vault. O'Brien, whose personal best was over 17 feet, set his opening height at his customary 15 feet, nine inches.

His first jump in the 94 degree heat was a miss. His second try was similarly poorly timed and he again failed to clear the bar. He still had his third attempt, but amid the heat, the pressure, and the prospects of failure, he missed a third and final time. He had to take a "no height," mathematically eliminating himself from any chance of qualifying for the U.S. team.

Scores of people complained. Surely

there had to be a way to let him try again? Other countries routinely gave waivers to world-class champions. (Ireland would later call to see if per chance Dan's father had been born on Irish soil). But the conclusion was as stable as that bar at 15-9. Dan O'Brien did not make the team. He did go to Barcelona – as a commentator for NBC Television. The man who was destined to become the next Bruce Jenner wound up sitting next to him … in the broadcast booth.

Reebok immediately pulled the ads.

Many mortals might have called it a career then and there. Particularly mortals already almost a decade beyond their college years. But anyone who saw what O'Brien did immediately following the pole vault debacle got a preview of his character. Instead of quitting or "dogging" the rest of the competition at the Trials, he competed to the bitter end.

Then, in September of 1992, a month beyond the bright lights of the Olympics, O'Brien quietly broke Daley Thompson's eight-year-old world decathlon record, scoring 8,891 points in a meet in France.

Just as quietly, he would bide his time until the Olympics came around again, four years later in Atlanta.

He first had to get past the U.S. Trials, of course, which he was able to manage in routine fashion. Just to be safe, he began at the lowest height in the pole vault, as a thousand media cameras captured his clearing.

In Atlanta, the pressure was as intense as the competition. A decathlete revival of sorts brought together one of the strongest fields in Olympic history, featuring, among others, Prark Buseman of Germany and Thomas Drovac of the Czech Republic, both with credentials capable of surpassing O'Brien. At the end of nine of the 10 events, O'Brien held a lead of 209 points over Buseman. If he could stay within 32 seconds of the German in the final event, the 1,500-meter run, he could clinch the gold medal. But it was far from a sure thing. Buseman's best 1,500-meter time for the year of 4:28.15 was some 44 seconds ahead of O'Brien's best of 5:12.01.

The German led by seven seconds after one lap and pushed hard to extend his lead, but although his final time of 4:31.41 was close to his personal best, O'Brien more than countered with a 4:45.89, eas-

ily his best time of the year.

At the finish line, Dan O'Brien raised his arms high in the air and wept openly as the crowd stood in ovation. More than anyone, Dan O'Brien knew the sweetness of a victory that had been a long time coming. ▼

ABOVE / *When the trip to Barcelona, a "sure thing," went down the tube, American Dan O'Brien looked fours years down the road for his redemption in the decathlon. And, in Atlanta, as the temperatures rose and the stakes climbed higher, O'Brien turned a lead going into the last event, the 1,500-meter run, into a sure thing.* ALLSPORT/M. POWELL

By anchoring the U.S. men's 5,000-meter short track relay team to a silver-medal finish in Lillehammer, Eric Flaim showed off his versatility. At the Calgary Games, he won a silver medal competing in the individual 1,500-meter long track event. ALLSPORT/BOTTERILL

Michael . Johnson

DOUBLE DARE

After all the waiting, after four years of running 300-meter sprints in the steamy Texas heat, after telling the world about his double dare and getting the Olympic schedule changed just to do it, after all the publicity and all the fuss, Michael Johnson stumbled.

Just after blasting from the blocks of the Olympic 200-meter dash final, the last step in his daring double, he faltered slightly, almost imperceptibly. Imagine Johnson's moment of panic. After losing a sure gold medal to a freak accident four years earlier, what if he lost another one the same way? What if he had fallen?

Johnson had learned the hard way that being the fastest, most dominating athlete on the planet was no guarantee in the Olympics. Tangled feet, a virus, a stumble, food poisoning – any of those things could wipe out years of work in a split second. Mary Slaney and Jim Ryun had tumbled to the track. Henry Marsh had turned up sick. Sergei Bubka had no-heighted. Michael Johnson had eaten the wrong meal.

Four years earlier, at the 1992 Olympics in Barcelona, Johnson was a sure thing in the 200-meter dash. A year earlier he

had won the 200 at the world championships. Earlier in the summer he won the Olympic Trials in a scorching 19.79. He had lost only two races in two years over 200 and 400 meters and ranked No. 1 in the world in both events. London bookmakers established Johnson as the surest bet in the entire Olympics to win a gold medal.

Little did they know that Johnson was

From 1968 to June 1996, the world record in the 200 had improved .11 of a second, 19.83 to 19.72, then Johnson ran 19.66. In a single night, Johnson improved it .34.

severely weakened by food poisoning. Two weeks before the Olympics, after running his final pre-Olympic race, he dined at a restaurant in Salamanca, Spain, with his agent, Brad Hunt. That night, his agent took sick. The next day it was Johnson's turn. He suffered for days. He dropped eight pounds, and with it went much of his strength.

If Johnson was uncertain how severely it would affect his performance, he learned

soon enough. In the first round at the Olympics, he ran a sluggish race, finishing in 20.80, and he knew he was in trouble. Observers thought he was taking it easy to conserve energy for the final, but Johnson knew it had taken all of his strength. In the second round he ran faster, 20.55, but finished second.

Then the almost unthinkable happened. Johnson finished sixth in his semifinal heat in a pedestrian 20.78; eleven men ran faster – men he had been whipping for years. Johnson not only would not win a gold medal, he wouldn't even qualify for the final. In the 4x400-meter relay, the U.S. set a world record, with Johnson running the slowest leg.

Who knew if Johnson would get another chance in the 200? A sprinter's shelf life is relatively short, and timing is everything. Joe DeLoach got hot in 1988, won the 200 in the Olympics, and was never heard from again. Johnson dominated the long sprints before and after the Olympics, but didn't have a medal to show for it.

During the next four years, he ruled the 200- and 400-meter dashes, and in 1993 he won the 400 at the world championships, giving him world titles in both sprints. He began to formulate a grand Olympic comeback. Why run just one race – the 400 or the 200 – and let an inferior sprinter win the other? Why not run both? No man had achieved the 200-400 double in a major meet since Maxie Long did it in 1899.

In 1995, Johnson won both races at the U.S. and world championships, narrowly missing world records in both. After months of negotiations, he finally convinced the IOC to change its schedule to accommodate his Olympic double.

He would make up for the '92 debacle and then some. "He carries that burn from '92," former college teammate Tony Miller told *Sports Illustrated*. "The only thing that'll cool him off is winning the double in Atlanta."

Johnson easily won the 400 in Atlanta, setting an Olympic record of 43.49. The 200 was expected to be more of a challenge. Two weeks before the Games, Frank Fredericks of Namibia had handed Johnson his first loss in two years.

Johnson cruised through the rounds, running 20.55 in the first, 20.37 in the second and 20.27 in the semifinals. This time he was conserving energy for the final.

As Johnson loaded himself into the blocks for the 200 final, he told himself, "This is the one I want, the one I wanted in Barcelona." The gun sounded and Johnson exploded from the blocks. Later he revealed that he actually stumbled three or four steps into the race and that it cost him a "few hundredths" of a second, but he remained upright and that was enough.

Johnson came off the curve slightly ahead of Fredericks, but he was just building speed. It was like red-lining a Ferrari in third gear and then jamming it into fourth. He exploded down the home-stretch.

"I saw (Bob) Beamon's jump (in the '68

Olympics) and before they measured it, one of the coaches I was sitting near said, I think we just saw something special," said Johnson's coach, Clyde Hart. "That's what it was like tonight. I knew it was special at 100 meters. But I thought maybe it would be 19.59 or 19.5-something."

The finish-line clock showed something beyond imagination: 19.32.

Ato Boldon, the bronze medalist, glanced at the clock and saw the time. Gosh, he thought, it's broken. Fredericks, the silver medalist, saw the clock and clapped like a fan. Ivan Garcia, another rival, bowed at the waist toward the winner.

What they had just seen was arguably the greatest single athletic feat in Olympic history, one that surpassed even Beamon's famous jump. It might be the equivalent of a nine-foot high jump, or a

31-foot long jump, or a 3:35 mile.

From 1968 to June 1996, the world record in the 200 had improved .11 of a second, 19.83 to 19.72, then Johnson ran 19.66. In a single night, Johnson improved it .34 – the largest single improvement ever. And he did it with virtually no wind, in heavy, humid air, at sea level, after running a total of 1 1/2 miles of sprints in six days.

"I knew I was running faster than I ever had in my life," said Johnson, who went to his knees at the finish and kissed the track. Four years later, he'd finally reached the end of the 200. ▼

ABOVE / *Michael Johnson cruised to a 200-meter semifinal victory, conserving his energy for the final. His clocking of 19.32 in the 200 smashed the world record and gave Johnson the 200-400 double.*

ALLSPORT/BRUTY

Competing for the Unified Team, Anfissa Restzova overcame three shooting mistakes with swift skiing and stormed to victory in the 7.5-kilometer race, beating silver medalist Antje Misersky of Germany by 15 seconds. **ALLSPORT/VANDYSTADT**

Vegard Ulvang quickly became the toast of Norway after plowing through the snowy Nordic courses at Les Saisies at Albertville to capture three gold medals and a silver.
ALLSPORT/COLE

For those properly positioned, the Olympics can provide a truly catapulting launch. ALLSPORT/VANDYSTADT

A Star is Born

They appear as if on cue, not taking over the Games as much as picking them up and lifting them higher. And then the Games lift back. One minute they're a hero in their own household, the next they're a hero in everyone's household. On the ship going over, or the plane, they're anonymous; on the ride home, they're already being swooped down on by shoe companies or Hollywood or the Ice Capades.

A lot has happened in between.

They are Jim Thorpe saying to Gustav V of Sweden, "Thanks, King;" they are Olga Korbut looking coy in Munich; they are Paavo Nurmi ignoring the crowd in Paris; they are Babe Didrikson winking at Clark Gable; they are Alberto Tomba calling home from a pay phone, collect, between runs; they are Bob Mathias hugging his mom in London; they are Toni Sailer borrowing a safety strap in Cortina; they are Oscar De La Hoya looking to the heavens in Barcelona.

They are as dissimilar as they are similar. But they all strike the same chord, a chord that combines opportunity with a terrific sense of timing. They know what *carpe diem* means. The result: stardom. Nothing more. Nothing less. They are Kip Keino beating the great Jim Ryun *in his prime*; they are Eric Heiden beating *everyone*; they are Dot Richardson hitting a home run after 18 years in the on-deck circle; they are Bonnie Blair and Al Oerter, athletes with the Midas, and the human, touch, each as perennial as the flame.

No matter where they go, no matter what they do, they are, in short, *Olympians*. Forevermore. ▼

Natalia Michkouteniok and Artour Dmitriev of the Unified Team display a graceful combination of strength and balance en route to the pairs gold medal in Albertville; two years later they again medaled, taking the silver after a memorable showdown with fellow Russians Ekaterina Gordeeva and the late Sergei Grinkov. ALLSPORT/BRUTY

Greg Louganis secured his place in the Olympic diving pantheon with men's platform and springboard gold medals in both Los Angeles and Seoul. ALLSPORT/DUFFY

J i m . T h o r p e

BRIGHT PATH BROKEN RULES

In the torch relay that carried the Olympic flame to the Centennial Olympic Games in Atlanta in 1996, the route was arranged so that the "flame from Olympia" would pass through the small Oklahoma farming town of Prague, in honor of former resident Jim Thorpe. The flame came and went in an instant. In terms of time, a small gesture. But symbolically the quick passage spoke volumes. Jim Thorpe, the first authentic Olympic legend of the modern era, was back in the fold.

It had been a long political haul, one that outlasted Thorpe himself. When he died in 1953 of a heart attack at the age of 64 he was still an Olympic pariah, his twin gold medals from the Stockholm Games of 1912 officially stricken from the books. He had broken the rules. Without telling anyone, he had sailed to Stockholm a professional due to the $60 a month he'd been paid to play baseball for a minor league team in North Carolina two summers before. Professionals couldn't win medals, and even if they somehow managed to col-

lect them, they sure couldn't keep them.

The "scandal" broke six months after Jim Thorpe towed home from Stockholm the winningest U.S. Olympic team ever.

No sooner did the Olympians disembark in New York than they were bombarded with ticker tape on Fifth Avenue. Standing tallest was Thorpe, the Native American (with a little Irish and French thrown in for good measure) from the Oklahoma reservation who had won both the one-day pentathlon (five events) and the three-day decathlon (ten events). In the decathlon, his performance – he won by nearly 700 points – was so conducive to gushing that the czar of Russia sent a 30-pound jewel-encased chalice to the awards ceremony, where King Gustav of Sweden proclaimed, "Sir, you are the greatest athlete in the world." To which Thorpe, whose Indian name was "Bright Path," replied, "Thanks, King."

Jim Thorpe was 24 years old and on top of the world. A man who counted royalty among his groupies. After the parades and the gifts, he returned to The Indian College in Carlisle, Pennsylvania, for his senior season of football, where he continued to be, well, Jim Thorpe. In a game against Army he ran 92 yards for a touchdown, had it called back because of a penalty, then ran 97 yards on the very next play for another touchdown. He scored 22 points in the win and 198 points for the season. He was named first team All-America for the second straight year, the best player ever to play for the legendary Pop Warner, Carlisle's coach.

It was after the football season that a newspaper in Massachusetts broke the news about the baseball-for-pay in 1909 and 1910. If the timing of the "scoop" was curious – had the news come earlier, he wouldn't have been able to play football at Carlisle – so was the ignorance feigned by Thorpe. "I was simply an Indian schoolboy ... I did not know I was doing wrong," he wrote to the head of the Amateur Athletic Union, James E. Sullivan. But then Thorpe exposed himself by pontificating that at least he didn't play baseball under an assumed name, as was the common practice of other college athletes of the era – common practice because, as they all knew, you couldn't play for pay and still compete as an amateur, no matter what the sport.

Indeed, for athletes wishing to remain

"pure" these were tricky times. The modern Olympics were founded on what was called the high moral ground of amateurism. "True sportsmen" were considered athletes who enthusiastically engaged in their "hobbies" but, still, neither devoted extraordinary gobs of time on them, or, worse yet, got paid money to do them. At least that was the theory – after a fifteen hundred year recess, the Olympics were still largely based in myth.

> ## King Gustav of Sweden proclaimed, "Sir, you are the greatest athlete in the world." To which Thorpe, whose Indian name was "Bright Path," replied, "Thanks, King."

But if such philosophy occupied the minds of the Olympic overseers, it was of no concern in 1909 and 1910 to Jim Thorpe, who by then had dropped out of college and didn't expect to go back. Play baseball for pay under his own name? Why not? If he'd heard of the Olympic Games, it was only barely. It wasn't until he was talked back to Carlisle for the 1911 football season – by Pop Warner, principally – that he was also talked into training for the Stockholm Games. "Heck," the coach told him, "You're such a natural you could win the all-around right now." This despite the fact Thorpe had never competed in an "all-around," or, for that matter, thrown a javelin,

which he didn't pick up until eight weeks before the Olympics.

The javelin, by point of fact, was his worst event in Stockholm. He finished fourth among the 29 decathletes. In every other event he was third, second or first. In the pentathlon, he was third in the javelin and first in every other event. King Gustav was not going out on a limb when he called Thorpe the world's greatest athlete.

Medalist or not, he remained an active athlete until his health went. He played baseball in the major leagues from 1913 through 1919, mostly with the New York Giants. After that, he was the first president of the National Football League when it opened its doors in 1920. In 1922 and 1923, he was player-coach of an all-Native American NFL team called the Oorang Indians; in 1929, he was still playing football, at the age of 41, for the NFL's Chicago Cardinals.

All the while, protests came and went concerning the Olympic medals taken away. For decades, the stance of the International Olympic Committee didn't budge. But gradually, over time, fantasies of amateurism gave way to the reality that athletes are athletes, pay or no pay. Finally, some 70 years after they'd been stripped from him – and 30 years after his death – Jim Thorpe's gold medals were returned to his family in January of 1983.

The error, they said, was "correctable." And in the summer of 1996, as the "flame from Olympia" passed through the small Oklahoma farming town of Prague on its way to Atlanta, those who were there said it seemed to flicker, in tribute to one of its own. ▼

OPPOSITE / *After Jim Thorpe won the pentathlon and decathlon in world-record style in Stockholm in 1912, there was little dispute that the 24-year-old American Indian was the greatest athlete in the world.*
ALLSPORT

Her smile tells it all: Seventeen-year-old Janet Evans, on loan from her senior year of high school, wowed the field in Seoul with three golds in three races; four years later she'd add another gold and a silver in Barcelona to become one of the most decorated U.S. female swimmers in history.

In 1984 in Sarajevo, East German Jens Weissflog won the gold in the normal hill ski jump and the silver in the large hill event, behind Finland's Matti Nykänen, who would win three gold medals in Calgary four years later. In Lillehammer, Weissflog, competing for Germany, resurfaced as a medal contender, winning two gold medals in the 120-meter hill and the team event.
ALLSPORT/VANDYSTADT

P a a v o . N u r m i

THE FINNISH LINE

His name is practically an Olympic synonym. Paavo Nurmi. The Flying Finn. The first of the multi-Games superstars. He competed in the three Olympiads of the roaring 20's – in Antwerp in 1920, in Paris in 1924 and finally in Amsterdam in 1928. And he fully planned, at the age of 35, to keep on running in a fourth Olympics, in 1932 in Los Angeles, but he was banned on the grounds that he was a professional because of the abundance of appearance fees he had accepted from race promoters around the world. Ironically, in the end, the Flying Finn stopped himself, a victim of his own high demand.

It's also a bit ironic that the achievement he is most known for, the one that has turned his name into an Olympic byword, is the sheer size of his medal collection. Paavo Nurmi won 12 medals in all, nine golds and three silvers, and to this day no one, not Jim Thorpe, not Jesse Owens, not Emil Zatopek, nor Carl Lewis, has matched that feat in men's track and field, the signature venue of the Olympic Games.

Winning a dozen medals is a noteworthy accomplishment, of course; but the overall number tends to overshadow what Nurmi did during three spectacular days in Paris in July of 1924, three days during which he won five of his nine gold medals while setting a pace that, to this day, remains astounding.

Those three days in Paris, *that* was Paavo Nurmi at his best – an unperturbable, relentless, consummate competitor. And if you threw an insult and a little hot weather in for good measure, so much the better.

He began his historic five-for-five run early in the afternoon of July 10 in Paris' Stade Colombes, where the stands were filled to overflowing with fans who had already, in days previous, seen Olympic records recorded by British runners Harold Abrahams at 100 meters and Eric Liddell at 400 meters. News of what Nurmi hoped to accomplish rebounded off the ivy-covered walls of the arena. His quest was to grab double wins that afternoon, first at 1,500 meters and then at 5,000 meters.

Nurmi's reputation as a "runner obsessed" preceded him. He made his mark four years previous in Antwerp,

> Paavo Nurmi won 12 medals in all, nine golds and three silvers, and to this day no one, not Jim Thorpe, not Jesse Owens, not Emil Zatopek, nor Carl Lewis, has matched that feat in men's track and field.

where he debuted inauspiciously with a silver medal in the 5,000 and then went on to win three straight golds, in two cross-country races as well as at 10,000 meters, where he avenged the loss in the 5,000 to France's Joseph Guillemot by setting such a blistering pace that the Frenchman crossed the finish line and threw up all over Nurmi's shoes. It wasn't just Nurmi's penchant for winning, however, that produced the intrigue that surrounded him. It was the stoical, almost antisocial, way he went about it. He barely acknowledged the cheering crowds, let alone his fellow competitors or photographers asking him to pose at the finish line. He was a reclusive, impenetrable Finn.

As a result, he didn't make a lot of friends. Well before the Paris Olympic Games, he had informed the French of his plans to double up in the 1,500 and the 5,000, hoping they would change their schedule. In sharp contrast to American sprinter Michael Johnson – who would pull off his historic double at 200 meters and 400 meters 72 years later in the 1996 Games after successfully lobbying the organizers to alter the schedule – the French declined to change anything for Nurmi.

They informed him that the races were scheduled to be run back-to-back, and they would be run back-to-back, with a half-hour in between.

The Finnish Olympic Committee intervened on Nurmi's behalf and managed to get a slight concession. An additional 55 minutes would be added for "rest time."

In the 1,500, Nurmi so dominated the field that he was able to ease up over the last 300 meters and still win in 3:52.6, a second off his own world record. After the race, as the crowd cheered, he didn't look at the stands as he picked up his sweater and left.

Eighty-five minutes later he was back, lined up for the 5,000, where, unlike the 1,500, he had a formidable challenger in the person of Vilho "Ville" Ritola, a fellow Finn who had spent the past four years in America, effectively dodging any showdowns with Nurmi while setting a world record at 10,000 meters. The Finnish officials had entered only Ritola in the 10,000 in Paris — which Ritola won in world-record time four days before the 5,000 — purposely leaving out Nurmi, the defending Olympic 10,000 champion, who they said was already entered in enough events. A development that didn't sit at all well with Nurmi.

As the gun went off to start the 5,000, Ritola, well aware that Nurmi had just run the 1,500, cranked up the pace. They went through the first thousand meters in a blistering 2:46, well ahead of world-record pace. But at the halfway mark Nurmi pulled ahead of Ritola by two meters and stayed there.

ABOVE / Some 70 years later, Finland's legendary runner Paavo Nurmi still leads the medal count with nine golds and three silvers in men's track and field. ALLSPORT

Ritola kicked hard down the stretch but the stubborn Nurmi, who refused to look at Ritola, kicked just as hard, keeping that two-stride lead across the finish line. He had his double.

At that, Nurmi was just beginning. Two days later he competed in the 10,000-meter cross-country race, an event run over and around the hills of Paris. The heat on the afternoon of July 12 was stifling, but the Stade Colombes crowd detected no suffering when Nurmi strode first into the stadium, wearing his usually expressionless expression. Only later, as the rest of the field emerged in various stages of heat exhaustion, about to collapse, did the heat's toll become obvious. Nurmi won by a full minute and 25 seconds over Ritola, and by nearly three minutes over the next finisher, as the distraught organizers decided then and there to discontinue cross-country as an Olympic event. It has not been seen since.

To put an exclamation point on his indomitability, a completely rested Nurmi returned to the track the next day to anchor Finland's triumphant 3,000-meter team with an 8:32 clocking, the best of the day by more than eight seconds.

His work in Paris completed, Paavo Nurmi collected his sweater and left the grounds. The Olympics had never seen anything like him ... and they haven't since. ▼

The signature venue of the Lillehammer Games was the cross-country course that meandered through a portion of the famed Birkenbeiner race course. Thousands of spectators jammed the scene daily, many of them arriving on skis themselves. **ALLSPORT/RONDEAU**

After Germany's Udo Quellmalz established himself as king of the half lightweight judo class (65 kg) in Atlanta, he received much more than a pat on the back.
ALLSPORT/BRUTY

Babe . Didrikson

YOU'VE COME A LONG WAY, BABE

ALLSPORT

No sooner had the 1932 Olympic Games ended in Los Angeles, California, than Grantland Rice, Paul Gallico, Westbrook Pegler and Braven Dyer – the four most famous sports writers in America – invited the star of those Games to join them for a round of golf.

Of course, Babe Didrikson agreed.

If sports were involved ... "She" always said yes.

Nicknamed for the most famous male home run hitter of all-time, more than half a century later Mildred Didrikson Zaharias remains an anomaly, an aberration. A female athlete so far beyond the crowd of her era, the crowd ceased to exist. As did the usual gender borders. Before she was through she would pitch an inning of exhibition baseball for the St. Louis Cardinals, she would play for the House of David barnstorming baseball team (the only one without a beard); she

Babe, a month beyond her 21st birthday, blew into Los Angeles, winked at Clark Gable, and announced, "I am going to beat everybody in sight."

would play as the only woman on an otherwise all-male basketball team called the "Babe Didrikson All-Americans," and she would enter a men's golf tournament in Los Angeles, where she would meet

her husband-to-be, professional wrestler George Zaharias.

But all that would come later, long after that round of golf with America's four most famous sports writers, each of them intrigued to get to know – and write about – this Babe who had just taken the L.A. Olympic Games by storm.

Which wasn't easy for a woman to do in 1932.

The jury was still out – way out – on whether a woman's place was on the track when Babe, a month beyond her 21st birthday, blew into Los Angeles, winked at Clark Gable, and announced, "I am going to beat everybody in sight."

Such brashness won her curiosity on the one hand and outright scorn on the other, particularly from her teammates on the U.S. Olympic Team, whose idea of athletic femininity during the fledgling days of female involvement – the Olympics didn't allow women to compete in track and field until 1928 – called for a more demure, if not outright humble, posture. Besides, her constant bragging hit their competitive nerves head-on.

But Babe – who could *really* get to her teammates when she boasted about the blue ribbon she won in the 1931 Texas State Fair for *sewing* – spoke loudly *and* carried a big stick. In her first event in Los Angeles, she threw the javelin 143 feet-4 inches to win by eight inches over the silver medalist and by nearly 20 feet over the next American.

Not that the U.S. "girls" hadn't seen it coming. A month before the L.A. Games, Babe had showed up at the AAU national championships/Olympic Trials as the lone member of the "team" representing the Employers Casualty Insurance Company of Dallas, Texas. She entered eight of the 10 women's events and, alongside more than 200 competitors, she took first place in six of them. She won the javelin, the shot put, the long jump, the baseball throw, the 80-meter hurdles, and she tied with Jean Shiley in the high jump. She also finished fourth in the discus. All by herself she scored 30 points, giving Employers Casualty the team title in a landslide. The University of Illinois women's track team, with 22 entrants, finished second with 22 points.

Because Olympic rules limited her to three events, Babe chose the javelin, hurdles and high jump for Los Angeles.

After opening with her gold-medal performance in the javelin – on one throw, total – Babe moved on to the hurdles, where she set a world record of 11.7 seconds, edging teammate Evelyne Hall, who finished a mere two inches back. Not only was Babe getting the best out of herself, but also out of all the women determined to beat her.

In the high jump, she and Shiley continued their battle from the trials. Both set a world record at 5-5 1/4 to close out the official jumps. In their jump-off, both women rose to yet another record height at 5-5 3/4. But although each would be credited with the world record – one that would stand for almost six years – the Olympic officials disqualified Babe for clearing the bar head first, an illegal maneuver in 1932. Babe reluctantly took the silver medal, saying she hadn't changed her jumping style in the slightest, and while there would be loud cries of political conspiracy – the girls finally got her – in the end, it wouldn't matter. In the heat of the Great Depression, Mildred Didrikson left the Los Angeles Olympics with two world records, two gold medals, and everyone wanting to meet her.

At first she starred in a vaudeville show, telling jokes, running on a treadmill and

playing her harmonica. She was greeted with sellout crowds, but show business isn't sports, and soon Babe drifted back to playing games. She played baseball and basketball with the men, but even that was too far from the real thing. Because of the income she generated through sports, her track and field career – strictly amateur in those days – ended in L.A., so she had no choice but to turn to a sport where she could honestly compete with other women.

She chose golf – that round with the sports writers gave her the bug, she said – and no one was surprised when she caught on quickly. After six months of lessons, she entered her first tournament, and won. In more than a decade of competition that included both professional and amateur events, she would win 82 tournaments, a total that included three U.S. Opens, both the United States and British Women's Amateurs, and, during one remarkable stretch, 17 wins in a

row in 1946. Frustrated by a lack of pro tournaments, she and her husband formed the Ladies Professional Golf Association – today's LPGA – in 1948. There were 11 charter members and 23 tournaments the first two seasons. Babe won 13 of them.

Not long after being named the greatest female athlete of the half century by the Associated Press – Jim Thorpe represented the men – she contracted cancer in 1953 and despite surgery and a comeback that included winning the 1954 U.S. Women's Golf Open, the cancer returned and she died in 1956. She was just 45 years old. ▾

ABOVE / *Olympic rules in 1932 limited the multi-talented, 21-year-old Babe Didrikson to three events. The American chose the javelin, the 80-meter hurdles and the high jump, winning the first two events and placing second in the high jump, only after the officials ruled her head-first jump illegal.*

ALLSPORT/IOC

Weighing 141 pounds, Turkey's "Pocket Hercules," Naim Suleymanoglu, staked his claim as maybe the greatest weightlifter ever after becoming the first lifter in Olympic history to win three consecutive gold medals. ALLSPORT/VANDYSTADT

The Germans came out like gangbusters and stole the team 100-kilometer competition in Barcelona, beating the Australians by nearly 1.5 seconds. ALLSPORT/VANDYSTADT

Australian distance swimming ace Kieren Perkins became only the third man in Olympic history to defend his 1,500-meter freestyle title when he duplicated his gold-medal winning performance in Barcelona with yet another golden performance in Atlanta. **ALLSPORT/BRUTY**

Bob . Mathias

GOLDEN SUMMER

By the time all was said and done, he would be the world record-holder and double Olympic gold-medalist in the decathlon, he would lead the Stanford football team to the Rose Bowl, he would be drafted by the Washington Redskins, he would become a Marine, he would win four terms as a United States Congressman from California, and he would even manage to get involved in an amateur-pro controversy after Hollywood paid him to play himself in The Bob Mathias Story.

Yet, if you want to hear the original Bob Mathias Story, the one that pre-dated the movie by a good five years, the one that captured the imagination of the entire world, the one that made real headlines, you have to go back to Tulare, Calif., population 12,000, in the middle of the hardscrabble San Juaquin Valley, in 1948. You have to go back to that day in mid-May, three weeks before Tulare High School would hold its graduation ceremonies, when Virgil Jackson, the track coach, approached his star senior athlete and said:

"Hey Bob, you ought to try the decathlon."

Thus began a most dizzying run of rags to Olympic riches, packed full of equal parts audacity, innocence and naivete. A run that wouldn't even take up the whole summer vacation, that began with a crash course in the decathlon, in May, in sunny California and ended with a final exam in August in London, England, in the rain.

As Bob Mathias himself would observe years later, sometimes it's better when you don't know what you're getting yourself into.

He was 17 years old when coach Jackson made his overture, a small-town athlete who starred in every sport he tried, including track and field, where he was a state champion high school hurdler. Despite the fact he'd never thrown a javelin, run a 1,500-meter race, or pole vaulted in his life – meaning he had exactly zero experience in thirty percent of the decathlon's 10 events – the coach wanted to enter Mathias in the Southern Pacific AAU decathlon championships on June 10, 1948 in Pasadena. Maybe, said Coach Jackson, riding a hunch, his high school star could earn a spot on the United States Olympic Team ... the 1952 team.

There was luck involved, of course, and good timing. This was 1948, after all, and the world, including the Olympic movement, was just beginning to shake off the downers of World War II. Many great athletes had seen their careers disappear with the war. There had been no Olympic Games for 12 long years, meaning a whole generation of kids – Bob Mathias' generation – had grown up without the Games. Many Olympic sports, principally track and field, had gone into a kind of limbo. A number of world records still dated back to the 1936 Berlin Olympic Games including Jesse Owens' sprint and long jump records and the decathlon record set by Glenn Morris.

In 1948 there were many athletes who, like Mathias, were just getting started.

But none got started any faster. In his first-ever decathlon at those Southern Pacific AAU championships in Pasadena, the 17-year-old won the competition. The completely unexpected victory qualified Mathias into the national AAU championships/Olympic Trials two weeks later in New Jersey, where the teenager from Tulare again prevailed, bettering, among others, three-time national champion Irving Mondschein.

When the *Queen Mary* set off from New York harbor for London in late July, carrying the United States Olympic Team, a bewildered Bob Mathias was on board.

He wasn't expected to win, or even medal, in London. In the face of world-class competition who knew just how fast the youngster might wilt?

It rained almost nonstop throughout the two days of the competition held in

That left only the pole vault, the javelin, and the 1,500-meter run – as fate would have it, the three events Mathias had "learned" just a little over two months ago.

London's Wembley Stadium, producing conditions hardly conducive to world-class performances.

But as the rain only got worse and the temperature dropped – and as his mother sat in the stands vowing she'd never let her little boy do this again – Bob Mathias refused ... to ... go ... away.

He didn't produce personal bests in every event, but neither did anyone else, and, in sharp contrast to the others, Mathias avoided disaster. All around him, his closest challengers found their waterloos, as it were. Enrique Kistenmacher, an army lieutenant and the pre-meet favorite from Argentina, was leading until he tripped in the sixth event, the high hurdles, and faded to a fourth-place finish overall; Mondschein,

who would finish eighth, and the other American, Floyd Simmons, the eventual bronze medalist, both suffered in the discus. If Simmons, in fact, hadn't gotten the lowest discus points of any medalist in Olympic history, he would have won the competition outright.

It wasn't until early evening of the second and final day of competition that Mathias, after the day's best discus throw, took over first place. That left only the pole vault, the javelin, and the 1,500-meter run – as fate would have it, the three events Mathias had "learned" just a little over two months ago.

First, as the officials shined a spotlight that showed, through the raindrops, where to plant his pole, Mathias cleared 11 feet, 5 3/4 inches in the pole vault, the second best effort of the day. After that, because the other group of decathletes had by now finished their competition, he knew he needed 786 points to surpass the score already accumulated by France's Ignace Heinrich, who would finish as the silver medalist. In the javelin, Mathias got 513 points. That meant he needed to finish the "metric mile" in less than six minutes. The 1,500 was hardly Mathias' best event, but six minutes was not too much to ask. He pushed himself to a 5:11, falling into a blanket held by his brother and his mother at the finish line.

When asked what he was going to do to celebrate, Mathias, two months out of high school and four years from the Helsinki Olympic Games, where he would finally break Glenn Morris' world decathlon record, looked out from the blanket long enough to answer, "I don't know. Start shaving, I guess." ▼

OPPOSITE / *Seventeen-year-old Bob Mathias won the decathlon in 1948 as a teen upstart, and in Helsinki four years later, the man to beat broke the world decathlon record.* ALLSPORT

Toni . Sailer

TRIPLE CROWN

The defining moment of the Toni Sailer Olympics – also known as the 1956 Olympic Winter Games in Cortina d'Ampezzo, Italy – came on the first day of competition at the skiing venue when Andreas Molterer of Austria recorded the fastest giant slalom time of the day and was mobbed by reporters and well-wishers at the finishing area.

"Wait," he said, holding up his hand and looking ominously back to the top of the mountain. "Toni has not yet come."

If anyone knew what Anton "Toni" Sailer was capable of, it was another Austrian. Molterer knew. Moments later, there came Sailer, slashing down the Ilio Colli course – named after a local Italian ski racer who had crashed into a tree and died – his body positioned perfectly, impervious to any danger. When he crossed the finish line, the mob indeed moved away from Molterer, now the holder of the silver medal, his time of 3:06.3 that had seemed sensational suddenly appearing quite pedestrian. Sailer had negotiated the course in 3:00.1, some 6.2 seconds faster – a margin of victory that still stands as the largest in Olympic alpine skiing history, and likely will stand forevermore in a sport where victories are typically determined by tenths of seconds.

Two days later, the "Dictator of the Dolomites" was at it again. Skiing against quick-turn specialists in the slalom, Sailer posted a two-run total of 3:14.7, four seconds ahead of Chiharu Igaya of Japan and nearly six seconds faster than the bronze medalist, Stig Sollander of Sweden. There were no repeaters in the top-six finishers from the giant slalom – with the exception of Toni Sailer.

Three days later, on a two-mile long downhill course as treacherous as any in Winter Games' history, Sailer had a chance to become the first skier to win all three alpine disciplines – giant slalom, slalom and downhill – in the same Games. By this time, none of his fellow competitors were betting against him. But then bad luck struck. As he stood near the starting gate, awaiting his turn to race, he reached down to tighten the leather safety straps that held his skis to his boots ... and one of them broke.

It was against the rules to ski without a safety strap, but Sailer had no spares. Nor did any of his teammates. As Sailer frantically searched for an extra strap, it seemed he would finally be beaten in Cortina – done in by a broken piece of leather.

Then, at the last moment, Hansl Senger, the trainer of the Italian team, attracted by the commotion in the Austrian camp, simply reached down and pulled a safety strap off his own ski. "Here," said Senger, "Take mine."

A grateful Sailer fastened the strap and was soon headed down a course where conditions bordered between bad and awful. The wind at the top was strong enough that it actually blew some skiers off course. In all, 28 of the 75 competitors would not finish, and eight of them would wind up in the hospital.

But Toni Sailer wasn't among them. He skied the course in 2:52.2 – 3.5 seconds faster than Raymond Fellay of Switzerland and four seconds ahead of his teammate Molterer. The highest-finishing Italian was Gino Burrini in sixth – meaning Senger, the good Samaritan, hadn't cost any of his team members a medal.

In all, Sailer won his three races en route to skiing's triple crown by 13.7 seconds,

> Decades later, it is still hard to explain why, and how, Sailer was able to so completely out-ski the world. Asked once to explain how he was able to win, he said simply, "I go faster."

an eon in ski time. By comparison, when French skier Jean-Claude Killy (who was inspired by Toni Sailer) won his triple crown at the Olympic Winter Games in Grenoble twelve years later, he prevailed by a combined 2.39 seconds – less than any one of Sailer's victories.

Decades later, it is still hard to explain why, and how, Sailer was able to so completely out-ski the world. He was the first perfecter of the *wedeln* technique of tail-wagging, but Sailer himself said *wedeln* was rarely a factor in racing gates. Asked once to explain how he was able to win, he said simply, "I go faster."

He was the quintessential European mountain man – raised in the heart of the Austrian Tyrolean Alps in the acclaimed skiing village of Kitzbuhel, where international ski racing began in 1933, two years before Toni was born. He worked in his father's glass shop and began skiing at the age of two. By 12 he was a promising local racer, influenced greatly by a friend of his sister's, Christian Pravda, who would go on to win a silver medal in the giant slalom and a bronze medal in the downhill at the 1952 Winter Games in Oslo. Sailer was determined to follow in Pravda's footsteps and become an Olympian himself.

Just two months beyond his 20th birthday when he came to Cortina, Sailer completely altered his life with his triple-crown performance. If he could do it all on the slopes, the world figured he could do it all away from the slopes as well. He gave it a good try.

After collecting his three gold medals – he gave one to his mom, one to his dad, and one to himself – along with the Golden Cross of Merit from the Austrian government and a nice plot of land in the heart of Kitzbuhel given to him outright by his grateful fellow villagers, Sailer branched out in all directions. Three years after Cortina he'd already become a movie star, with five movies to his credit in two countries (Austria and Japan),

he'd written an autobiography (over 200,000 in sales in French, German and Japanese), he'd marketed a fiberglass ski (price tag in 1955: $135), he'd cut some records, he'd come out with his own line of stretch pants (Sailer-Tex), and he'd opened his four-story, 32-room inn (Haus Toni Sailer) on the land he'd been given in Kitzbuhel.

After making his mark, and a pile of money, Sailer – who lost his amateur status because of his movie and endorsement deals – settled mostly into running the inn. In 1972 he took over as head of the Austrian Ski Team, which had fallen

on hard times, and – to no one's surprise – led a resurgence back to the top. ▼

ABOVE / *In 1956 at Cortina d'Ampezzo, Italy, Austrian Toni Sailer became the first skier to win all three alpine disciplines – giant slalom, slalom and downhill – in the same Games.* ALLSPORT

Carl Lewis made the Olympic team by an inch, then made the Olympic final on his last attempt, and produced only one jump good enough to medal, but it was good enough to win his fourth gold medal in the long jump at the age of 35. ALLSPORT/M. POWELL

*A great leap for Nigeria: Long
jumper Chioma Ajunwa soars to
gold in Atlanta.* **ALLSPORT/DUFFY**

U.S. long jumper Mike Powell brought the world record and a giant-killing reputation with him to the Olympic Games in Barcelona. It was Powell who, in 1991, broke the record set by Bob Beamon's legendary jump in the Mexico City Games of 1968. Alas, in Barcelona, as in Seoul four years earlier, Powell ran into the long Olympic shadow of Carl Lewis, and settled for silver medals to Lewis at both meets.

ALLSPORT/BRUTY

A l . O e r t e r

If THERE'S A WILL, THERE'S A WAY

In many ways, the discus throw is the quintessential Olympic event. Dating back centuries, it bridges the gap between the ancient and the modern Olympics. Statues as far back as the 3rd century, A.D., immortalize not the swimmer or the sprinter or the tennis player, but a discus thrower. If Michelangelo's David were an athlete, he would have thrown the discus. Athenians and Spartans threw the discus. It takes a real athlete to throw the discus. It takes coordination, timing, skill, concentration, technique and dedication. And it doesn't hurt to be strong as a bull.

And if the discus throw is pure Olympic sport, then Al Oerter is as pure an Olympic athlete as the modern Olympic Games has yet to produce. From Melbourne in 1956 to Mexico City in 1968 – a span of four straight Olympic Games – Oerter won the discus gold medal every time, setting an Olympic record every time. And every time he

was favored to lose. In retrospect, the story seems almost made up.

Al Oerter was a perpetual Olympic underdog. Although at times he held the world record, he never entered the Olympic Games with that distinction. He was never at his peak prior to an Olympics. And worse yet, most of the time he managed to hurt himself, seriously hurt himself, just before the competition. And yet he always won. An entire generation of world-class discus throwers might still be in psychotherapy

> It takes a
> real athlete to throw
> the discus.
> It takes coordination,
> timing, skill,
> concentration,
> technique and
> dedication.
> And it doesn't hurt
> to be strong as a bull.

over Al Oerter. The man who once said, "You die before you don't compete in the Olympics" always found a will and a way to win.

The phenomenon began when Oerter was in high school. As the story goes, one day a discus landed by his feet during track practice. Oerter was a sprinter on the team. He picked up the discus and heaved it back to his teammates, and

missed them by at least 40 feet when his throw sailed over their heads. The coach saw the incident and a career was born.

Oerter wound up going to the University of Kansas on an academic scholarship. In the 1956 NCAA championships he placed fourth. And in the National AAU tournament he managed sixth. Hardly the signs of an Olympian, let alone a gold medalist. But Oerter still somehow managed to make the 1956 U.S. team headed for Melbourne, Australia, along with Fortune Gordien, the world record-holder.

Then, with no one paying attention to this 20-year-old American college student, and with nerves so bad he could hardly keep them under control, Oerter's very first throw sailed beyond the flag marking the Olympic record. At 180-6 1/2 , it was by far the longest throw of his life. It would also turn out to be the longest throw of the competition. No one caught him, not Gordien, not Italy's 1948 gold medalist, Adolpho Consolini. It had taken just one throw to put Al Oerter's name into the Olympic record book.

Four years later in 1960 at Rome's Stadio Olympico, Oerter was a well-known world-class discus thrower, but ranked only second on his own team. American Rink Babka had beaten Oerter at the Olympic Trials and threw 190-4 on his first throw at Rome. Oerter had five chances to beat him. His first was hopeful – 189-1, but then came 186-1 1/2 , followed by 185-5 1/2 and then 186-1 1/2. Finally, with only one throw to go, Al Oerter chucked the discus farther than he'd ever thrown it before. He beat Babka by four feet. Gold medal number two.

During the three years following the

Rome Games, Oerter came into his prime as a discus thrower, winning impressively at international meets around the world and setting the world record several times. But just before the 1964 Olympic Games in Tokyo he injured a disk in his neck and his throwing was painful and erratic. He had a special brace built to try to ease the pain as he threw. He lost to Jay Silvester in the U.S. Olympic Trials and watched as Czechoslovakia's Ludwig Danek amazed the discus throwing world with a world-record toss of 211-9 1/2 just prior to the start of the Games.

With only six days left before the Games, Oerter fell during practice and tore his rib cage. His doctors told him not to participate at all in Tokyo, but Oerter waved them off. It was in this setting that he uttered his famous, "You die before you don't compete in the Olympics."

Danek led convincingly after the first four rounds in Tokyo and everyone had more or less counted Oerter, what with the body harness and ice packs, out. But after four weak throws, Oerter landed an amazing throw that flew past them all – 200-1 1/2 to be exact ... for gold medal number three.

In 1968 at Mexico City, Oerter was 32 years old and it appeared he was washed up. He was coming off the worst competitive year of his life. He managed just fourth place at the American AAU championships and at the U.S. Olympic Trials he placed far behind Silvester and Gary Carlson, who was on a roll, setting world records with a huge 218-3 1/2 throw in Modesto, California, and an even longer 224-5 in Reno, Nevada. Going into the 1968 Games, five discus throwers around the world had throws beyond Oerter's personal best.

At Mexico City, Silvester promptly broke the Olympic record in the qualification round with a throw of 207-9 1/2. But then big Al Oerter found from somewhere within his 6-foot-4, 260-pound frame a monster throw. He beat Silvester by almost five feet. Another Olympic record and gold medal number four.

Al Oerter became the first person to win four consecutive gold medals in any Olympic track and field event. He will be 68 years old at the start of the Sydney Olympic Games in 2000 and he reportedly has no plans to enter the competition. But if he did, no one would count him out. ▼

ABOVE / *The story of discus thrower Al Oerter: Four Olympic Games, four comebacks, four gold medals, four Olympic records.* ALLSPORT

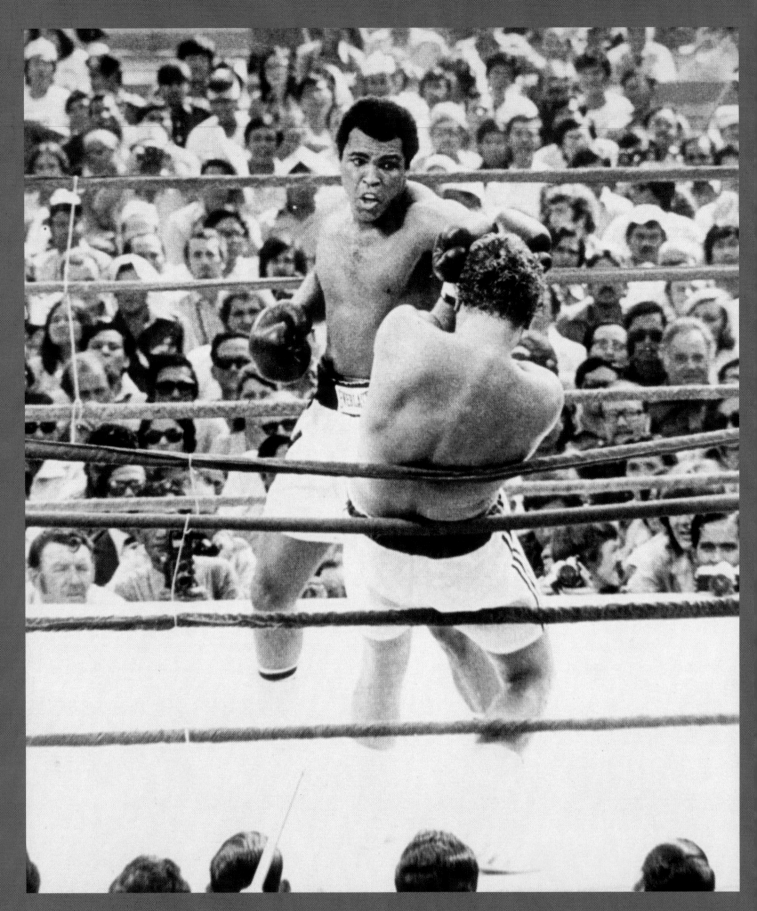

It was the Olympic Games that launched boxer Muhammad Ali to his status as The Greatest (ALLSPORT); at the Centennial Games in Atlanta, The Greatest was feted by, among others, members of the United States Dream Team. ALLSPORT/PENSINGER

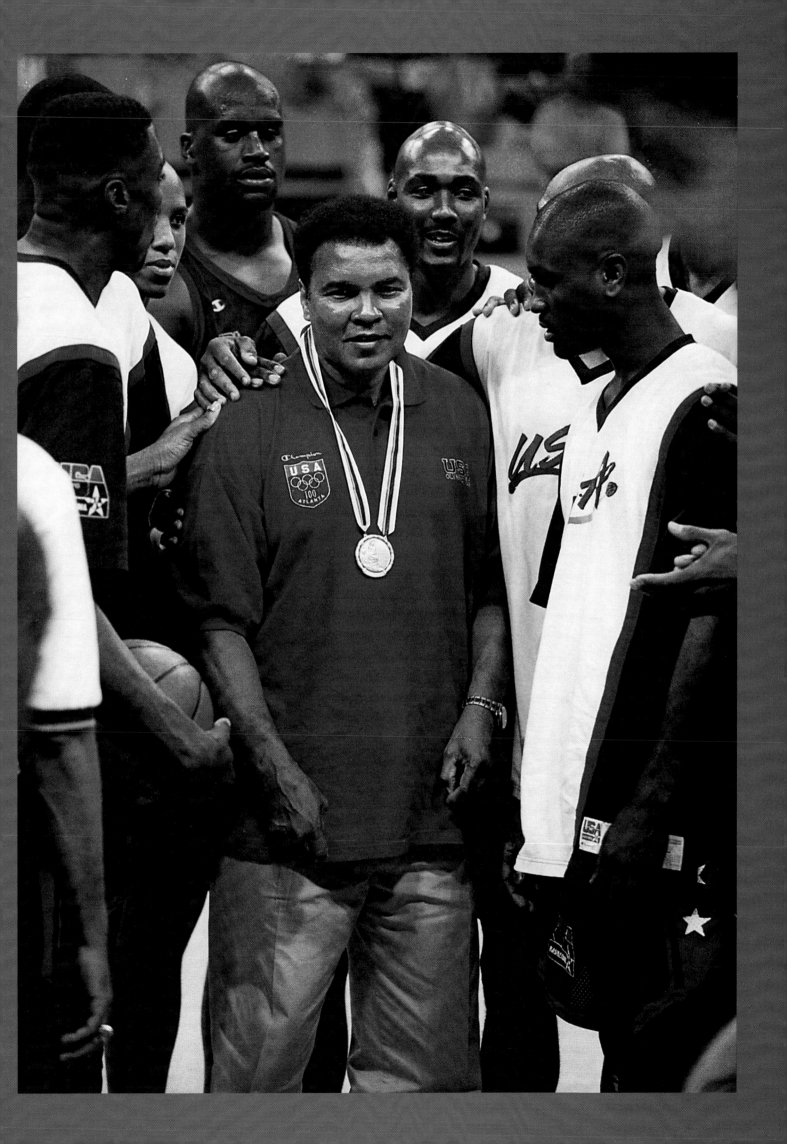

Kipchoge Keino

DERAILING THE RYUN EXPRESS

Kenya's Kipchoge Keino may not be the most accomplished of Africa's long and impressive string of great middle- and long-distance runners who have emerged since the African running revolution was launched after Ethiopian Abebe Bikila showed up in Rome in 1960 and won the marathon in bare feet. While Keino's total Olympic haul of four medals in three Olympic Games, including two golds and two silvers, is impressive enough, other African runners have won as many and more.

But with the possible exception of Bikila, Keino's timing is second to none. It was Keino who showed up at the starting line in Mexico City in 1968 to challenge the speediest and best-known miler of the 20th century, the supposedly indomitable Jim Ryun of the United States. And it was Keino who, as hundreds of millions around the world watched on television, held off Ryun's patented and ferocious kick on the final straightaway until Ryun sputterred away and the Kenyan won by

nearly three seconds, the largest margin of victory in Olympic metric mile history.

The giant-killing triumph would stamp the policeman from Kenya with fame forevermore.

Again in 1972, Keino proved to be Jim Ryun's nemesis, although this time inadvertently. Lumped together in the fourth opening heat of the 1,500, Keino burst safely to the front of the qualifiers as Ryun tangled himself in a bunched-up

crowd and tripped, falling to the track and failing even to qualify for the final. Footage of that race was played and replayed, with images that again reflected the '68 result – showing the Kenyan running in front and the star-crossed American far behind. Far more people wound up scrutinizing that heat than the 1,500-meter final held the next day – when Keino faded down the stretch and

finished second by three meters to Finland's Pekka Vasala. But the loss hardly seemed to matter. By that time, Keino – who had already won the 3,000-meter steeplechase in those 1972 Munich Games and would go on to place second in the 5,000-meter run – had already reaffirmed his reputation as the man who derailed the Ryun Express.

As milers and metric milers go, certainly few have been bigger game than Jim

> At the age of 16, when back in Kansas Jim Ryun was six weeks from entering the "sub-four" club, Kip Keino's best time in the mile was, at 5:49, barely a shade under six minutes.

Ryun. A phenom since becoming the first high schooler to break four minutes as a 17-year-old Kansas schoolboy in 1963, Ryun came into the 1968 Olympics with an unbeaten streak in both the mile and the 1,500 that stretched for more than three years. As the world record-holder at the three marquee distances of 880 yards, 1,500 meters and the mile, the 21-year-old American was the undisputed king of the middle distances. There is little surprise that the man who toppled him would gain wide acclaim.

It didn't hurt that Kip Keino's story was fascinating in its own right. The world's press soon plugged into his upbringing, which was far from the Olympic norm. Hezekiah Kipchoge Keino was raised as a Nandi, a branch of the Kalenjin Tribe, one of the 38 major tribes that inhabit Kenya. His mother died when he was four and after that he was raised alternately by a kind grandmother, an abusive uncle and an absentee father, himself a runner of

note, although hardly as a member of the organized running fraternity. Keino herded goats as a ten-year-old, was chased by leopards, was raised almost solely on fruits, vegetables, milk and "a little blood," ran constantly in the mountainous valleys of his homeland, a mile and more above sea level, and wasn't developed and refined as a runner until he joined the national police force at the rather advanced age of 18. Indeed, at the age of 16, when back in Kansas Jim Ryun was six weeks from entering the "sub-

four" club, Kip Keino's best time in the mile was, at 5:49, barely a shade under six minutes.

For a Kenyan, however, the Kip Keino story was hardly unique. Most of the Kenyans who burst on the running scene in the early 60's were, like Keino, "late developers," most, too, were from either the Kalenjin or Kisii high-mountain tribes; most had grown up drinking vats of milk, and, if pressed, most could come up with a story involving a leopard.

Keino wasn't the first Kenyan to medal in the Olympics, either. That honor belonged to Wilson Kiprugut, a bronze medalist at 800 meters in 1964 in Tokyo, where Keino's best effort as a 24-year-old first-time Olympian was fifth place in the 5,000 (along with an elimination in the semifinals from the 1,500).

Kiprugut's would be the lone Kenyan medal in Tokyo. But four years later, amid Mexico City's familiar thin air at 7,800 feet, the oxygen-conserving Kenyans fairly exploded onto the scene. Besides Keino's win in the 1,500, two other

Kenyans — Amos Biwott in the steeplechase and Naftali Temu in the 10,000 meters — won gold medals and no less than eight Kenyans and 12 Africans overall won medals in seven separate running events — an amazing progression considering that Abebe Bikila's marathon gold medal in Rome, captured a scant eight years earlier, was the first-ever gold medal, at any distance, for an African.

Literally dozens of African runners, and especially Kenyans, have won medals in the Olympic Games since. They have commandeered events such as the steeplechase practically as their own. In Seoul in 1988, Barcelona in 1992 and Atlanta in 1996, Kenyans collected seven of the nine available steeplechase medals, losing only a bronze in '88 and another bronze in '96. In the 5,000- and 10,000-meter races and in the marathon, Kenyan medalists have been commonplace.

And yet, the most famous name, easily the most recognizable, among Kenyan Olympians continues to be Kipchoge Keino. Not only was he at the beginning of the wave, but he was a runner who had an uncanny knack for bursting out in front whenever the great Jim Ryun — who never did, as it turned out, win an Olympic medal, of any color — happened also to be in the picture. ▼

LEFT / *Down the homestretch in the 1,500 meters in Munich, Finland's Pekka Vasala (in blue) exploded, Kipchoge Keino faded to second and the legendary Jim Ryun, having tangled, tripped, and fallen in the qualifying race, never started.* ALLSPORT

OPPOSITE / *Kenya's Kipchoge Keino's claim to fame is not his medal count — two golds and two silvers in three Olympics — rather it is whom he beat in the thin air of Mexico City: America's best-known miler Jim Ryun. In Mexico, Keino gives a hug to another Kenyan gold medalist, Naftali Temu, who won the 10,000 meters.* ALLSPORT

Russia's answer to Wonder Woman: In 10 career Olympic events, Ljubov Egorova medaled nine times, including five golds. En route to the five-kilometer gold medal, Egorova holds her tuck in Lillehammer.
ALLSPORT/BRUNSKILL

O l g a   K o r b u t

MIGHTY SPRITE

When Olga Korbut entered the athletes' village in Munich in August of 1972, she was as unknown to the world as any given pole vaulter from Liechtenstein or Mongolia. By the time she left three weeks later, she was the best known athlete of the Games – and she had turned the sport of women's gymnastics from its former ballet-like performances by mature women into a sport of fun and games for little girls.

Not bad for an alternate.

Officially, that's how Olga Korbut's Olympic career began: as a reserve on the star-studded team from the Union of Soviet Socialist Republics; the seventh member of a six-woman squad. The plan was to use her sparingly, if at all. She was just 17 — young by contemporary women's gymnastics standards, and she had never before performed in a major international meet. Like the rest of the Soviet team members, she was in the shadow of the great Lyudmilla Tourisheva, winner of the all-around gold medal at the previous Olympics and the acknowledged star of the Soviet show.

But Olga did find her way into the line-up in Munich – and a sport would never

be the same as a result.

It wasn't so much what this pig-tailed redhead went on to accomplish, three

gold medals and a silver, it was how she did it that turned the world, free and not free, into her personal fan club – and sent unprecedented numbers of little girls from Kiev to Tokyo to Atlanta looking for the local gymnastics hall.

She had all the exuberance, and showed all the emotion, of the teenager she was, and the world loved it, and they loved Olga, all 85 pounds and four feet, eleven inches of her. All by herself, with not a trace of premeditation, she personalized herself and her sport, and just for a little while during the Cold War that was at its peak in 1972, she cracked the facade of the stern and menacing bear that was the Soviet Union. Richard Nixon later remarked that her performance in Munich "did more for reducing the tension during the Cold War than the embassies were able to do in five years."

For there, on worldwide television, was one of the Soviet Union's own, laughing and crying and failing and winning, and doing it all with the unabashed enthusiasm that only a teenage extrovert can bring to the stage. She had a smile as big as Red Square itself and an individualism more reminiscent of Teddy Roosevelt than Vladimir Lenin.

Her routines were anything but routine. She did a backward flip off the balance beam, something no one had ever done before in international competition, and she was acrobatic and poised. She charmingly played to the audience during her floor exercise, and performed seemingly death-defying stunts on the uneven bars. Some purists immediately loathed her, calling her performance a circus act, and her own country would later openly criticize her free spirit, but mostly people just watched, in unheard-of numbers for women's gymnastics, captivated by this fresh face of the Soviet Union.

Olga was first discovered at Munich during the team competition, where, along with her teammates, she collected her first gold medal and caused something of a stir with a dazzling and daring performance on the uneven bars. But it was during the all-around competition that the worldwide audience really took

notice of her. Word spread quickly that this charming youngster from Grodno, near Minsk, was in striking distance of winning the gold medal, of beating her own teammate, Tourisheva, and East Germany's highly regarded Karen Janz.

At the all-around's halfway mark she was in first place and hundreds of millions of people tuned in as she took her turn on the uneven bars – the same event that had dazzled the judges only two days before in the team competition. Olga

> ## What Sonia Henie had done for ice skating, Olga Korbut did for gymnastics. There were less than 15,000 American female gymnasts in 1972. Two years later, there were more than 50,000.

went for broke – and broke. She stumbled on the mount, slipped on the bars, and fumbled the dismount. She received a disastrous 7.5 and dropped out of contention, eventually taking seventh place. She made her way to her seat in Olympiapark Sporthalle and right there in front of a worldwide audience cried her eyes out. And everyone felt her pain, and adopted her as their own.

As the competition continued with the individual apparatus competitions, she triumphed anew with a stirring comeback. She won the gold medal on the balance beam, added a silver on the uneven parallel bars, and concluded with an unforgettable floor exercise routine performed to the music of the German World War II film, *The Woman of My Dreams*. She mixed acrobatic somersaults with pure gymnastics and just a touch of Radio City Music Hall. She winked, she smiled and she flirted, and the crowd went wild. The judges gave her a 9.90 and the gold medal, just ahead of the technical perfection of Tourisheva.

The public's fascination with her grew by leaps and bounds. She received more than 20,000 telegrams. She was invited to Disneyland, given a new car (which the Soviet Sports Authority wouldn't let her keep) and returned home to Minsk a bona fide international star. She was named 1972's Female Athlete of the Year by the Associated Press and virtually every other association in the world.

What Sonia Henie had done for ice skating, Olga Korbut did for gymnastics. There were less than 15,000 American female gymnasts in 1972. Two years later, there were more than 50,000. All around the globe, thousands of young girls turned their attention to gymnastics, all wanting to be the next Olga Korbut. A little 10-year-old girl in Romania was one of these *wannabes* and an exuberant West Virginia pre-schooler was another. Later, Nadia Comaneci and Mary Lou Retton would have their turns, but in 1972 it was Olga Korbut, all by herself. ▼

OPPOSITE / *Pig-tailed Olga Korbut was a dancing ray of sunshine among the stern facade of the Soviet Union Olympic machine in Montreal. She won three golds – in the team event, the balance beam and the floor exercise – and tied for the silver in the uneven bars.* ALLSPORT

Eyes on the prize: U.S. archers Justin Huish, Butch Johnson and Rod White shot straight and true to claim gold in the men's team event in Atlanta, outscoring the Koreans, 251-249. ALLSPORT/BILOW

Eric . Heiden

SWEET SWEEP

He had just dusted off the last obstacle standing in his way – and that's putting it politely. What Eric Heiden did to the world of speed skating from Feb. 15 through Feb. 23, 1980, at the Olympic Winter Games in Lake Placid, New York, might more accurately be described as *demolished*. He started with a win at 500 meters, followed that a day later with a win at 5,000 meters, followed that with a win at 1,000 meters, won yet again two days after that at 1,500 meters, and finally, with a *coup de grace* on the closing day of the Games, hammered down in the 10,000-meter endurance race, adding devastation to domination with not just a win, but a win in world-record time. In Olympic speed skating history, no one had ever swept the distances ... won 'em all ... run the gamut from the sprints to the stamina races. Not until him.

Now he had nothing left to fear but fame itself.

It was the only race he didn't want to skate: the rat race. Whatever Eric Heiden's motivations for ruling the world, none of them, it would soon become obvious, were about glory. Or fortune. Or celebrity. After he'd been in

the spotlight for all of about 15 minutes, he had this observation: "It's kind of a drag ... I liked it better when I was a nobody."

The day before the Lake Placid Games began, in other words.

Prior to the 1980 Olympic Games, only the world of speed skating knew who Eric Heiden was. And as worlds go, they don't get much more remote than speed skating.

> Even Heiden's massive legs – with a 32-inch waist and 29-inch thighs, they barely tapered until below the knee – couldn't be expected to bounce from speed to stamina and back again.

It's not that speed skaters are reclusive by design, it's just that the sport has enough built-in geographic limitations to lend itself to anonymity. Its practitioners are primarily people who not only have access to a constant supply of ice, but to smooth ice. A handful of northern countries – Norway, Sweden, Finland, Holland and Russia among them – traditionally develop the most, and the best, speed

skaters. In the United States, an icy pocket in the northern midwest – with Madison, Wisconsin, serving as a kind of unofficial Mecca – has been known to produce its fair share as well.

Eric Heiden grew up in Madison.

He was fast enough as a 17-year-old to skate for the United States in the 1976 Winter Games in Innsbruck, where he placed seventh in the 1,500 and 19th in the 5,000. Just one of the crowd. But that would be the last time. A year later, by now a seasoned 18-year-old, he won the overall title at the 1977 world championships. In 1978, ditto. In 1979, ditto again. As a 21-year-old coming into the 1980 Winter Games – with the competition on USA ice – he was definitely the favorite.

But, even so, he wasn't considered *unbeatable*.

There were too many events, too close together, at too wide a range of distances, to think that any human could run the table.

In speed skating, as in running, there is a definite distinction between the shorter and longer distances. The sprints call for quick, anaerobic bursts, the body requiring every available quick twitch muscle fiber. The distances, on the other hand, call for systematic, aerobic pacing, requiring slow twitch muscle fiber.

Rare are the legs that can handle both. Even Heiden's massive legs – with a 32-inch waist and 29-inch thighs, they barely tapered until below the knee – couldn't be expected to bounce from speed to stamina and back again as the *race du jour* might demand.

The closest any Olympic speed skater had come to a sweep was in 1924 in Chamonix, where Finland's Clas Thunberg won the 1,500 and the 5,000, placed second in the 10,000 and third in the 500; and in 1972 in Sapporo, where Ard Schenk, the Flying Dutchman, won golds at 1,500, 5,000 and 10,000 – but stayed out of the 500 completely.

Beyond the imposing physical constraints against going five-for-five in Lake Placid (a fifth event, the 1,000-meter race, had been added to the Olympic program in 1976), Heiden also faced a formidable field. Among the entrants in the 500 –

Heiden's weakest event – were Yevgeny Kulikov of the Soviet Union, the world record-holder and defending Olympic champion, and Heiden's U.S. teammate, Tom Plant, who a week before the Olympics had beaten him in the 500. In the 5,000, Heiden would have to get past current record-holder Kai Arne Stenshjemmet of Norway; and in the 10,000 yet another world record-holder, Soviet skater Viktor Leskin, was in the field.

But on the first day of Olympic competition, Heiden served notice early by winning the 500. Paired with Kulikov, he

pulled away on the final straightaway to win in Olympic record time.

When he followed the next day with a win in the 5,000, relegating Stenshjemmet to second place, people began to talk. Then, after holding serve in the 1,000 and 1,500 – he was already the world record-holder at both distances – he found himself standing on the threshold of history in the 10,000.

To help set the stage, the night before the 10,000 Heiden went to the U.S.-U.S.S.R. hockey match and watched history unfold on another front as the underdog Americans pulled out a most improbable 4-3 victory. Inspired by the fervor of his countrymen – and frightened after watching the supposedly invincible Soviets go down to defeat – Heiden showed up for the 10,000 the next morning and quickly took care of business as he made sure of victory by lowering the world record by nearly six seconds.

He retired undefeated, electing, at 21, to hang up his skates and move on to new, less visible, challenges. He became a serious cyclist and was an alternate on the national team before turning pro. In 1986 he cycled in the Tour de France, happily tucked away in the *peloton*, just another *domestique*. After that he enrolled in the Stanford Medical School, in the hopes that he could follow in his father's footsteps and become an orthopedic surgeon. "I always wanted to be a doctor," he explained at the time. "I knew when I was a young athlete I was going to have to rely on my brain someday." In 1991, at the age of 33, Eric Heiden got his medical degree. No one doubted that he would. ▼

LEFT / *At Lake Placid, Eric Heiden already held the world record in the 1,000- and 1,500-meter distances, but his five-for-five gold-medal performances included beating the three world-record holders at 500, 5,000 and 10,000 meters.* ALLSPORT/DUFFY

Hello Mary Lou! Mary Lou Retton made history as the first American woman gymnast to win the women's all-around after a spirited duel in Los Angeles with Romania's Ecaterina Szabo. ALLSPORT/S. POWELL

The body language of U.S. gymnasts Bart Connor and Peter Vidmar leaves no doubt as to the outcome of the men's team competition in Los Angeles. The title was the first for American men since the 1904 Games in St. Louis, when every team entered was from the U.S. ALLSPORT/S. POWELL

Oscar . De . La . Hoya

FOR MY MOM

L ike a lot of other youths growing up in East Los Angeles, Oscar De La Hoya got in a lot of fights. Fortunately for his opponents, they were with 10-ounce gloves and headgear.

A tough kid in a tough neighborhood, De La Hoya could easily have chosen a different way to grow up. Gangs were all around him. Drugs were readily available. Guns were commonplace. Dropping out of school was as popular as crack cocaine. Drive-by shootings were becoming a regular feature of neighborhood life and the crime rate was constantly on the rise. This was Los Angeles in the 1970s and 1980s, where life had a way of knocking young men down, and keeping them there.

Oscar De La Hoya chose a different route than many of his contemporaries for two reasons. His mom and his dad.

From his earliest years, De La Hoya's parents urged him to work hard, be honest, and stay in school. And if he had any aggression he wanted to release, take it on down to the boxing gym. Cecilia De La Hoya, a native of Mexico, taught her son integrity and character. Joel De La Hoya, a former club boxer, taught his son

Cecilia De La Hoya, a native of Mexico, taught her son integrity and character.
Joel De La Hoya, a former club boxer, taught his son how to throw a punch.

how to throw a punch. They were the original Team De La Hoya.

Oscar started boxing at the age of six. By the time he was in high school, he was obsessed with the sport. He would attend Garfield High School by day and the Dame Boxing Club at night. He was up every morning at 5 a.m. to put in an hour of running before school. He went to bed early. For three hours every evening, Oscar honed his boxing skills at the gym. Adopting his father's advice – and style – he became an outstanding straight-ahead fighter, never backing up, always going forward. The kid had no reverse gear. A hard, no-nonsense puncher, he became regarded as one of the city's most promising young boxers.

De La Hoya's amateur career took off like a rocket. At the age of 15, he won the 1988 Junior Olympic title. The next year he won the championship at the prestigious Goodwill Games and compiled an impressive amateur record of 167 wins against only four losses. Enormously popular with all ages of people, the personable De La Hoya was the pride of East Los Angeles, his following all-encompassing. On one occasion, he was robbed by five young men in an East L.A. barrio. They stole his wallet containing his identification and one hundred and fifty dollars in cash. Later that evening, the wallet was anonymously returned to the front porch of the De La Hoya home, the money undisturbed.

De La Hoya's skills in the ring were matched only by the goals he set. After the win at the Goodwill Games, his main desire was to win an Olympic gold medal. As a seven-year-old boxing novice he had soaked up the thrills of the 1984 Los Angeles Olympics, especially the boxing matches in the Sports Arena in downtown L.A., not far from his home.

After the Olympics, he determined that he would turn professional and become the lightweight champion of the world. He told his mother about these teenage dreams and she enthusiastically approved. They talked about Oscar's goals often.

Then, suddenly, just as Oscar's training indicated the dream had a chance of becoming reality, Cecilia De La Hoya died. She was just 38 years old when cancer took her life in 1990. Before she died, Oscar promised his mother he would win a gold medal for her at the Olympic Games.

The next year, 1991, with an amateur record that had increased to 223 wins with only five losses, De La Hoya entered the biggest international meet of his life at the World Championships in Sydney, Australia. This was to be a preview of the following year's Olympic Games scheduled for Barcelona, Spain. By this time, people were heralding De La Hoya as the next Sugar Ray Leonard — the effervescent American boxing star of the Montreal Olympic Games. Like Sugar Ray, De La Hoya was seen as a boxer with style in and out of the ring. He was the heavy favorite to win the world title.

But he didn't. Marco Rudolph, a tough hotel chef from Germany, out-pointed the favored De La Hoya, 17-13, in a preliminary round match. Rudolph then went on to capture the title. Suddenly, Oscar De La Hoya wasn't so invincible any more. He would still be taking his Olympic dream to Barcelona, but now he would enter the competition as some-

thing other than a sure thing.

In Barcelona, De La Hoya scored impressive victories in the opening rounds before barely surviving an 11-10 decision over South Korea's Hong Sung-sik in the semifinals. Then, as fate would have it, De La Hoya met his old foe Marco Rudolph in the gold-medal final. The only obstacle standing between him and the fulfillment of his Olympic dream — not to mention his promise to his dying mother — was this world champion from Germany.

After two rounds De La Hoya held a slim one-point edge. In the third and final round, the young American ended the fight by knocking Rudolph down with 1:09 remaining. The fight was stopped and De La Hoya was awarded the gold medal — the only American boxer to earn gold at the Barcelona Games. The American flag was raised at the award ceremony. But Oscar De La Hoya, the man on the top step, held two flags, one American, for his homeland, and the

other Mexican, for his mother's.

De La Hoya flew home a celebrity, a popular boxer made much more so by his Olympic win. In great demand for public appearances, he was immediately scheduled as a guest on the Tonight Show. But before any of that, he returned to East Los Angeles and laid his Olympic gold medal on his mother's grave. ▼

In Barcelona, Oscar De La Hoya brought home the only gold for the U.S. team, which had its poorest showing — three medals — in 26 years.

ALLSPORT/M. POWELL

A provocative routine performed to the music of Bach elevated the previously conservative ice dancing pair of Marina Klimova and Sergei Ponomarenko from the Unified Team to a surprise gold medal in Albertville. **ALLSPORT/MARTIN**

Bonnie Blair

SCALING THE 39-SECOND WALL

B onnie Blair did not become a speed skater for the money. For one thing, there is no money in speed skating. Speed skating has about as much money as Parcheesi. For another thing, Bonnie Blair was only two years old when she started skating, and you don't do anything for money at the age of two. You do what your family does. And for the Blairs of Champaign, Illinois, that meant skating. The youngest child of Charles and Eleanor Blair didn't really have any choice in the matter.

This was a girl who can't remember whether walking came before or after skating. On the day Bonnie Blair was born, her dad was running the timer at a local skating meet. He learned of his daughter's birth when the news was announced over the public address system. Bonnie wasn't just the baby of the family, she was more like the skating caboose. Her family nickname was "one of the gang." She wore more hand-me-

down ice skates than the junior hockey league. She entered her first skating competition at the ripe old age of four, on her big sister's skates.

Bonnie Blair did not stay with competitive speed skating for the fame and glory, either. Speed skating has only slightly more fame and glory than it has money. True story: Even after becoming arguably America's most famous speed skater in history, the name "Bonnie Blair" was a clue on *Jeopardy!*, the popular television

months at a time, she pushed her body to peak performance by endless hours of biking and running and weightlifting, all for the love of the competition and the sport. She personally oversaw the raising of $7,000 at the age of 19 so she could enter her first Winter Games in Sarajevo in 1984. It was a far cry from the state funds that propped up the East Germany speed skaters who dominated the sport – and who were heroes in their homeland – at the time.

She could hardly believe her eyes. 38.99. She basked in the glory of finally achieving that elusive goal, of establishing a new world record, of dipping under 39 seconds.

game show that's very purpose is to stump people. (Her name, by the way, was the correct answer to the question: *Who is America's top female speed skater?*).

The simple truth, as Bonnie Blair explained after every one of her Olympic medals and after each of her four appearances in the Olympic Winter Games, was that she became a speed skater – and she remained a speed skater – because of her love for the sport. That was the short answer and the long answer. There was never any other explanation, or motivation, beyond that.

She trained year-in, year-out, for 30 years because of her genuine enjoyment of the sport. She paid her own way to European meets, she lived away from her family for

In her Sarajevo debut, Bonnie did not medal, but she took eighth in the 500 meters behind a "Who's who" list of speed skaters from behind the Iron Curtain, led by East Germany's world record-holder Christa Rothenburger.

Four years later, at the Calgary Winter Games, Rothenburger again dazzled the world with her performance in the 500 meters, breaking her own world record with a time of 39.12 seconds. With that, however, she only took second place. First place went to Bonnie Blair of the United States who finished in a blistering and world-record clocking of 39.10 seconds – a time tantalizingly close to breaking the vaunted 39-second barrier, a long elusive goal of all women 500-

meter sprinters. At the same Games, Blair also won the bronze medal in the 1,000-meter sprint.

By now an Olympic veteran, Blair came to the 1992 Winter Games in Albertville as the favorite. She did not disappoint, winning gold medals at both 500 meters, with a time of 40.33, and 1,000 meters, with a 1:21.90 clocking.

By the time the Lillehammer Winter Games rolled around two years later, Blair was 29 years old and planning to retire at the end of the next international skating season. This, then, would be her final Olympics. As an added bonus, if she could duplicate her Albertville "double" and win at both 500 and 1,000 meters, she could become the first U.S. female Olympian, summer or winter, to win five gold medals.

Again, Bonnie did not disappoint. After opening with a win at 1,000 meters she then won her third consecutive gold medal at 500 meters with a time of 39.25, once again teasing, but not scaling, the 39-second wall.

In spite of her rather obscure chosen sport, and in spite of her best efforts to downplay what she had done, after Lillehammer Bonnie and her five medals did indeed become a genuine celebrity. She met with the President — at his request. She made the rounds of the television talk shows. She threw out the opening pitch at a Chicago Cubs baseball game. She was named *Sports Illustrated's* Sportswoman of the Year for 1994. She was on the cover of TIME magazine. She was on the Kelloggs' Corn Flakes box.

But, as Bonnie Blair would be the first to tell you, fame is fleeting ... especially for speed skaters.

Post-Lillehammer, Blair participated, as she had promised, in a final year of competition. During that year, she returned to Calgary, the scene of her first gold-medal victory where a packed Olympic audience had watched enthralled.

Now, at thirty, she assembled with the other world-class racers for the 500-meter finale, waiting her turn. When the gun sounded for her pair, she got off to one of the best starts of her career. She blazed across the finish line far ahead of her competitor. She looked quickly at the scoreboard to check her winning time. She could hardly believe her eyes. 38.99. She had finally done it. The feeling was overwhelming. She loved it. She basked in the glory of finally achieving that elusive goal, of establishing a world record, of dipping under 39 seconds.

There were fifty people in the stands. ▼

ABOVE / *America's favorite speed skater, Bonnie Blair finally broke the 39-second barrier in the 500 meters, not at the Olympic Games with a sold-out cheering crowd, but one year after Lillehammer at the world championships where a gathering of 50 people watched the world-record race.* ALLSPORT/M.POWELL

Nicknamed La Gazelle by the French press, Marie-Jose Perec strode to a double 200- and 400-meter victory in Atlanta.

ALLSPORT/HEWITT

Donovan Bailey was pumped after his victory in the 100-meter dash in Atlanta, in which he established a world record of 9.84, well below his previous best of 9.91.

A l b e r t o   T o m b a

TOMBA LA BOMBA

Every time he skied he put on a clinic. His body perfectly positioned at angles custom-fit for the split-second turns required by his craft. His skis quiet but moving incredibly fast. His path efficient, his movement controlled yet explosive.

But more than his legendary skiing style, Alberto Tomba burst on the scene like no skier in the history of the Olympic Games because of his personal style. As good as he was at ski racing, his personality provided even a better story. *La Bomba Tomba*. Tomba the Bomb. Thus he was christened when he showed up for his first Olympic Winter Games at the age of 21 in Calgary in 1988 and thus he would remain, a man who could completely command the room.

It took him, oh, about a minute to crash the party.

In a Calgary Winter Games that already had its fair share of characters – there was Eddie "The Eagle" Edwards, the ski jumper from England whose goal was

"not to die;" there was the Jamaican Bobsled team – it was Tomba, a largely unknown World Cup rookie, who managed to upstage them all. No sooner had he skied to more than a second lead after the first run in his first race, the giant slalom, than he took off his skis, walked to a pay phone, and called his parents back home in Bologna, Italy. Within full view of a small army of reporters, Tomba talked to his father, Franco, a wealthy clothing store owner, and reminded him of his promise to buy his son a new Ferrari should he win Olympic gold.

When he hung up the phone, *La Bomba* said to the reporters, "I told him I wanted a red one."

A media star was born.

True to his expectations, Tomba proceeded to win his first gold medal – and

Ferrari – with more than a second to spare.

In the slalom two days later, he showed he could also win by coming from behind. Tomba was in third position after the opening run, but in an all-out second run he overtook the field.

In an Olympic career that would go on to span three more Winter Games, from Albertville to Nagano, Tomba would continue to do everything but put on the brakes.

At Albertville in 1992, he became the first alpine skier to win gold medals in the same event twice when he prevailed over World Cup legend Marc Girardelli in the giant slalom. Two days after that he had a chance to make yet more history by becoming the first Olympic alpinist to win four gold medals – but finished second in the slalom to Norway's Finn Christian Jagge. At that, La Bomba left them shaking their heads in awe. He was 1.58 seconds behind Jagge after the first run, a deficit that bordered on eternal in ski racing time, but in the second run he blistered down the course and made up so much ground that he actually stood in the gold-medal position with only Jagge left to race. The nervous Norwegian skied 1.3 seconds slower than Tomba, but his overall time was still .28 of a second faster and he just managed to hold off the Italian for the gold.

At Lillehammer in 1994, Tomba won a silver medal in the slalom – a one-medal haul considerably less majestic than his previous Olympic collections. But again, he provided all the suspense. After an opening slalom run that was more than a second behind the leader, Austria's Thomas Stangassinger, Tomba pulled an Albertville déjà vu when he skied a second run that was nearly a full second faster than Stangassinger. Still, it wasn't quite enough. In combined time, he wound up losing to the Austrian by 15 hundredths of a second.

As dramatic as the racing was, it was never the whole Tomba story. *La Bomba* never stood still when he took his skis off, either. While he was becoming the most decorated alpine skier in Olympic history he was also becoming the most public and flamboyant one. In Calgary, no sooner had the news of his red Ferrari died down than it became public that he had asked Katarina Witt of Germany, the defending women's figure skating gold medalist, out

on a date ... and Witt had turned him down. In Albertville, he delayed his entrance until just before his first main event, the giant slalom, and then arrived from the Italian Alps by helicopter, proclaiming to the thousands of fans who had driven to the Games from Italy that a name change – to Alberto-ville – was in order. In Lillehammer, he showed up engaged to a former Miss Italy, but pub-

An Olympic day with Alberto Tomba in it was never dull, or slow. He never met a situation he couldn't, and wouldn't, turn into a party.

licly announced that he was still willing to give Witt – back in the Olympics for the first time since Calgary now that professionals were eligible to skate – a chance.

Besides having good times, Tomba was the ambassador of the good time. An

Olympic day with Alberto Tomba in it was never dull, or slow. He never met a situation he couldn't, and wouldn't, turn into a party – a legacy perhaps best characterized by an incident that occurred in the aftermath of the slalom race at Albertville, where the hard-charging Tomba's second run nonetheless relegated him to second place behind Jagge, the Norwegian – a finish that denied Tomba a place in history as the first skier to win four gold medals.

It was enough of a disappointment that no one would have been surprised if it had been received with a certain amount of soberness and restraint. But as the last of the 119 entrants skied through the ruts to conclude the event, a Costa Rican skier named Alejandro Preinfalk Lavagni made Olympic history of sorts by taking nearly two and a half minutes to negotiate the slalom course – a time believed to easily be the slowest ever recorded.

When Lavagni finally skied across the finish line, there to enthusiastically greet him was Tomba, who, along with goldmedalist Jagge, hoisted the Costa Rican to their shoulders and turned and bowed to the roaring crowd. ▼

Emotions run the gamut in the Summer and Winter Games, be it a win, lose or draw situation ...

... In Barcelona, they (like everyone else) lost to the Dream Team, 127-76, but the Lithuanians celebrated perhaps more than just a victory on the court when they beat the Unified Team, 82-78, for the bronze medal. ALLSPORT/M. POWELL

... An exhausted, ice encrusted Silvio Fauner savors his moment of victory as anchor of the Italian team in the men's Nordic 4x10-kilometer relay in Lillehammer. ALLSPORT/VANDYSTADT

... The women's Canadian relay team endures some anxious moments track side in Seoul. ALLSPORT/MORTIMORE

OPPOSITE / After Florence Griffith Joyner had literally run away from the field in both the 100- and 200-meter sprints in Seoul, Jamaican sprinter Grace Jackson said of the record-breaking American sprinter, "She runs a different race than we do." ALLSPORT/M. POWELL

D o t . R i c h a r d s o n

WORTH ITS WAIT IN GOLD

Not even Hollywood could have written Dot Richardson's story any better than real life. In a wrap: A child softball star turns down a professional team, postpones a lucrative medical career, collects a mountain of debts and wakes the neighbors with her incessant late-night batting practice in her apartment, all just to wait and prepare for an Olympic moment that might never come.

By the time she finally gets her wish, she is 34 and the oldest player on the team. She opens the Olympics by hitting the first Olympic homer and she closes them by hitting another homer that clinches the gold medal — a shot that, as Hollywood would have had it, barely misses hooking foul. Fade out with a celebration. Roll the credits.

Dorothy Richardson was Roy Hobbs come to life, the Natural coming back late in life to claim the dreams of her youth.

"My three big Olympic dreams happened," she gushed afterward. "The first was to hit a home run in my first Olympic at-bat — well, it came on my fourth. The second was to hit a home run in the gold-medal game. The third was to be on the

ABOVE / *There was no one more ready to play ball than 34-year-old Dot Richardson when softball was officially placed on the Olympic roster in Atlanta. With an impressive 111-1 record in international play and an undefeated pre-Olympic barnstorm tour (pictured), the American women were billed as "The Other Dream Team" in Atlanta and they did not disappoint.* ALLSPORT/SQUIRE

podium to get the gold medal."

For once, life seemed to be fair. Was there anyone more deserving of such a performance? Was patience, determination and hard work ever so justly rewarded?

Even her youth was the stuff of Hollywood fluff. Legend has it that one day a boys' Little League coach saw her playing ball and invited her to join his team on the condition that she cut her hair and change her name to Bob. No thanks, she said.

Instead, at the age of 13, she became the youngest player ever to play on the Orlando Rebels of the ASA women's league. In 1976, at 15, she was drafted by a professional softball team, but she refused the offer because she wanted to preserve her amateur standing so she could play in the Olympics someday. Little did she know that she would have to wait two decades.

Richardson spent the prime years of her athletic life on hold while the Olympics ignored her sport. Softball was fine for family reunions and company picnics, but not for the Olympics. The sport began its Olympic lobby in 1965. It was finally considered for inclusion as a demonstration sport for Seoul in 1988, but ultimately passed over.

Meanwhile, Richardson played softball for UCLA, where she became a four-time All-American (her performance earned her the honor of being named the NCAA Player of the Decade for the 80s). Following her collegiate career, she attended the Louisville medical school, but continued to play softball. She was named the outstanding defensive player in the ASA women's major fast pitch league seven times.

Softball was again considered for inclusion as a demonstration sport for the 1992 Olympics, but once more was passed over. In 1994, Richardson began to give up her Olympic aspirations and

started surgical residency at the USC Medical Center. But just as she was beginning a new profession, softball was given medal status for '96.

Richardson took a leave of absence from her residency to train. She set up a batting cage in her apartment and practiced late into the night until a neighbor left a note on her door one day: "Please, train for the Olympics at an earlier time." She taped the barrel of the bat to muffle the sound and continued her practice.

For Richardson, it also was something of a gamble. "Do you know how much those hands are worth?" a surgeon friend asked her once. That was enough to get her to

"I'm $140,000 in debt," Richardson once noted, "but there's no price you can put on making an Olympic team."

change her head-first slide to feet-first.

"I'm $140,000 in debt," Richardson once noted, "but there's no price you can put on making an Olympic team."

It was a momentous occasion for softball aficionados when their sport finally made its Olympic debut. They mailed formal invitations to the nation's media – "After waiting 29 years, seven months, 21 days and nine hours," the announcement said, softball would make its debut in the Atlanta Olympic Games, albeit 105 miles away in Columbus. Softball had waited even longer than Dot Richardson to get into the Olympics.

It probably was no coincidence that the

Americans happened to have a pretty fair softball team, which certainly could explain their zeal in lobbying the IOC for Olympic inclusion. They were billed as The Other Dream Team in Atlanta and boasted a 111-1 record in international play the previous 10 years.

Nobody anticipated softball's debut more than Richardson did. She woke up twice the night before the first game hoping it was time to play. As Hollywood would have had it, Richardson wore No. 1, batted No. 1, hit the first hit, scored the first run and slugged the first home run in Olympic softball history in Game No. 1. She triggered the *coup de grace* of a 10-0 rout in the sixth inning. For months she had told her teammates and parents that she'd had repeated dreams of hitting a home run in her first Olympic game.

The Americans, cheered by sellout crowds of 8,500, breezed through the first five games of the tournament, but then suffered a shocking 10th-inning, 1-0 loss to Australia. In that game, American Lisa Fernandez threw a perfect game for nine innings and teammate Dani Tyler hit a home run that didn't count because she failed to touch home plate.

But the U.S. bounced back and met China in the championship final. First Richardson stopped the Chinese with her arm. With two Chinese runners on base in the top of the third inning of a scoreless game, Richardson, the shortstop, killed the rally by throwing out a base runner at home plate. Then in the bottom of the inning she beat the Chinese with her bat. Richardson hit a sharp blast down the right-field line with a runner on base. The ball curved right and cleared the fence and the foul pole for a home run – her third of the Olympics. The U.S. got one more run that inning and held on for a 3-1 gold-medal winning victory.

"The wait was worth it," said Richardson. "It was too long ... But I loved it." ▼

With picture-perfect long-jumping form, Jackie Joyner-Kersee leapt her way into the Olympic record books with two gold medals ('88, '92) and one silver ('84) in the heptathlon and a gold in the long jump in Seoul in 1988, followed by two bronzes in Barcelona and Atlanta.

Ukraine's Inessa Kravets outlasted a
Russian and Czech to claim triple jump
gold in Atlanta. ALLSPORT/ M. POWELL

As illustrated by this airborne skier in the
Albertville Games of 1992, the legacy of
the Olympic Games, past, present and
future, is a perfect blend of pageantry and
intensity. ALLSPORT/M. POWELL